Start-Up Multiculturalism

Integrate the Canadian cultural reality in your classroom!

Cindy Bailey

Pembroke Publishers Limited

© 1991 Pembroke Publishers Limited
538 Hood Road
Markham, Ontario
L3R 3K9

Pembroke Publishers gratefully acknowledges the financial assistance of the Secretary of State for Multiculturalism in the production of this book.

Canadian Cataloguing in Publication Data
Bailey, Cindy
  Start-up multiculturalism

Includes bibliographical references.
ISBN 0-921217-63-3

1. Multiculturalism – Study and teaching (Elementary) – Canada.* 2. Multiculturalism – Canada – Problems, exercises, etc.* I. Title.

FC104.B35 1991   372.83   C91-094039-8
F1035.A1B35 1991

Editor: Penny Fine
Design: John Zehethofer
Cover Photography: Ajay Photographics
Typesetting: Jay Tee Graphics Ltd.

Printed and bound in Canada
9 8 7 6 5 4 3 2

ACKNOWLEDGEMENTS

Every effort has been made to acknowledge all sources of material used in this book. The publishers would be grateful if any errors or omissions were pointed out, so that they may be corrected.

Black Line Masters #4, 5, 6, 7, 8 and 9
Courtesy of Policy and Research Multiculturalism. Department of the Secretary of State. Multiculturalism and Citizenship.

Black Line Masters #2, 10, 11, 12, 14, 15, and 16
Excerpted from the *Alberta People Kit* and provided courtesy of:
The Alberta Multicultural Commission, (formerly the Alberta Cultural Heritage Foundation)
Gene Zwozdesky, Project Director,
2nd Floor, 12431 — Stony Plain Road,
Edmonton, Alberta
T5N 3N3.
(403) 427-2927

Black Line Masters #21, 22 and 23
Excerpted from the *Alberta People Kit* and provided courtesy of:
The Alberta Multicultural Commission, (formerly the Alberta Cultural Heritage Foundation)
Gene Zwozdesky, Project Director,
2nd Floor, 12431 — Stony Plain Road,
Edmonton, Alberta
T5N 3N3
(403) 427-2928
Adapted from *Multicultural Teaching: A Handbook of Activities, Information and Resources* by Pamela L. Tiedt and Iris M. Tiedt. Allyn and Bacon, Inc. Boston. 1979.

Black Line Masters #26 and #27

Reproduced from Protestant Moral and Religious Education, Level 5, Government of Quebec, Elementary Curriculum Guide.

Introduction 5

       How to Use START-UP MULTICULTURALISM 6
       General Tips 7
       Glossary 8

Social Studies and Multiculturalism 11

       Activity #1   Who Am I? 12
       Activity #2   Our Needs, Our Cultures 13
       Activity #3   Our Origins, Our Backgrounds, Our Family Trees 14
       Activity #4   Family Ties 17
       Activity #5   Our Places of Origin 18
       Activity #6   The Sum of Our Parts 19
       Activity #7   Join Us and Share 20
       Activity #8   Why Immigrate? Who Is an Immigrant? What Is
                     It Like? 21
       Activity #9   Tracing Our Time Lines, Discovering Our Roots 24

Language Arts and Multiculturalism 25

       Activity #10 Introducing Ourselves 26
       Activity #11 Our Names 26
       Activity #12 How Our Names Are Chosen 27
       Activity #13 My Autobiography 28
       Activity #14 Our Neighbourhood 30
       Activity #15 Families 33
       Activity #16 Feeling Different 35
       Activity #17 How We Can Help 37
       Activity #18 Discrimination 38
       Activity #19 New Canadians 39
       Activity #20 Calendars 41
       Activity #21 Is this Fair? Does Justice Prevail? 43
       Activity #22 Telling Our Own Tales 44
       Activity #23 Justice and Injustice in the News 45

Values and Religious Education and Multiculturalism 46

       Activity #24 Canada's Religious Mosaic 47
       Activity #25 Our Religious Practices 48
       Activity #26 My Religious Tradition 49
       Activity #27 Visiting Houses of Worship 49
       Activity #28 Similar and Different 50
       Activity #29 Are We Really Different? 52
       Activity #30 Case Studies 53
       Activity #31 Defending Our Rights 53

Appendix 55
       Black Line Masters 56
       Annotated Resource List 96

Start-up Multiculturalism would not have been developed without the support and continuous encouragement of the St. Lawrence Protestant School Board Parents' Committee and the South Shore Protestant Regional School Board (S.S.P.R.S.B.), Quebec. Furthermore, the financial assistance from the Department of the Secretary of State, Multiculturalism and Citizenship, allowed me to take the time needed to research and prepare the guide for my fellow teachers.

In particular, I wish to gratefully acknowledge Mrs. Anne Heath, Chairperson of the Parents' Committee, who ensured parental involvement in this multicultural education initiative. Mr. Robin Drake and Mr. William Green, Directors of Elementary Education at the S.S.P.R.S.B., ensured the Board's financial and pedagogical commitment to the project.

I also want to thank Mr. William Johnson, the Director General of the S.S.P.R.S.B. for his full support of the project and confidence in my work.

I wish to thank all the teachers and students in the various schools across Canada who helped in the field-testing and thereby made this guide work in the classroom.

Dr. Charles Ungerleider of the Faculty of Education, University of British Columbia, did the final review of this guide and I gratefully acknowledge his revisions and suggestions.

A special acknowledgement must go to Jan Andrews, my editor and advisor, who out of a personal commitment to multiculturalism and to the education of young children, gave me both inspiration and support to write-up the many drafts and re-drafts of this guide.

Last but not least, I wish to thank Nicole Ross, my typist, who patiently worked through the manuscript till it held together as a whole.

Introduction

Increasingly, it is becoming accepted that multiculturalism must play an important part in the educational experience offered to all Canadian students. Why?

— Because multiculturalism is the way that we, as Canadians, have chosen to deal with the fact that all of us, without exception, have roots in different times and traditions;

— Because multiculturalism provides us with a means to ensure that none of our heritages shall be given precedence; that each shall be encouraged to achieve full development. It gives us the fabric out of which we weave our lives.

But educators have received little help or direction bringing multiculturalism into the classroom. And so, in order to meet the needs of the children in my classroom, I began to develop the strategies which eventually became START-UP MULTICULTURALISM. The Quebec Ministry of Education Curriculum for Elementary Schools was my starting point for an integrated approach to multiculturalism in education. Eventually, this guide was pilot tested in more than 100 classrooms across the country. The results of this process, along with suggestions from professional reviewers, have been incorporated into this guide to ensure that it has widespread applicability.

This guide presents an integrated approach to multiculturalism. It is not designed to be used in isolation, but rather to be worked into the existing framework of studies — Social Studies, Language Arts, Values and Religious Education and, by extension, areas such as Visual and Dramatic Arts.

The emphasis throughout is on methodology. While teachers will use a wide range of resources as they implement the activities, they will not need to spend a lot of time in extensive prior study. They can quickly get involved in using the materials and can, along with their students, use the scope that this approach provides, for personal and academic growth.

Those who have worked with START-UP MULTICULTURALISM recognize that it has limitations; it does not offer answers to every difficulty or respond to every challenge pertaining to integrating multiculturalism into the curriculum. Teachers are asked to use it in that spirit, keeping alert to further work that may be needed and to changes they themselves must make. This one publication will not change the world, but with it, we hope that you will make your "world" more reflective of its citizens, your students.

The overall aims of START-UP MULTICULTURALISM are to enable students to:

— grow personally in pride in themselves and in respect and acceptance of others;
— recognize the importance of their role in building a society of harmony and individual and collective growth;
— understand the multicultural nature of Canada.

Outreach is a very important element in this approach to multiculturalism. Children are asked to seek out information in their own homes and families. Members of the community are invited into the classroom to exchange knowledge, give demonstrations or simply experience the activities. This approach, which was chosen to supplement inadequate resources, has had unexpected, very encouraging results. We have seen ties within families, and beyond, strengthened. As parents contribute to school life, their confidence and involvement has grown. Reaching out into the home and community is essential in achieving the aims of this guide.

What will teachers need to use START-UP MULTICULTURALISM? Perhaps most importantly, the flexibility to listen to students and learn from them; to follow the leads that they offer; to make use of unforeseen opportunities; and to know that numberless exciting chances lie ready within reach. Teachers will also need the sensitivity to accept that people behave, respond and believe in different ways; that every human situation involves common needs and human feelings.

Beyond that? A commitment to the knowledge that multiculturalism is not just an issue for new immigrants or for members of visible minority groups. It belongs to all of us. It is our heritage.

How to Use Start-Up Multiculturalism

As previously noted, this guide is not intended to replace existing curricula. It should be used in conjunction with regular programmes of study, by integrating activities into lessons, as appropriate.

START-UP MULTICULTURALISM is a practical "how-to". Emphasis is on methodology, rather than on "teaching the teacher". Nonetheless, the many print and audio visual resources described in the Annotated Resource List will extend the knowledge of both students and teachers alike.

The glossary, included at the beginning should be used as a continuing reference. Return to it and expand upon it as issues crucial to an understanding of multiculturalism are explored.

The framework consists of three sections, corresponding to three curriculum areas:

Social Studies
Language Arts
Values and Religious Education

Introductions to each section describe the major concerns, objectives and relevance to multiculturalism of the curriculum area.

Each section is divided into themes. Themes consist of a series of activities. START-UP MULTICULTURALISM is not designed to be used in a strict linear fashion. Teachers may sequence the sections, themes and activities to meet the needs of their students and programme.

Activities contain the following elements:

— A descriptive title
— Two lists of objectives describing student learning outcomes (1) Multicultural objectives and (2) Skill objectives
— A list of resources required to carry out the activity. These include books, audio-visual materials, Black Line Masters, family and community members. Those activities which require very specific resources include alternative suggestions for those who cannot find the resources. The list is not intended to be restrictive; teachers should alter and add to it to meet their needs and reflect their experience.
— Detailed procedures describe how to carry out the activities. A full range of strategies are suggested, including group and individual work, class discussion, written and oral projects. Again, teachers should allow activities to develop according to student needs and potential.
— Some activities are followed by extended activities, which provide opportunities for further exploration through more intensive study, demonstrations, crafts and visual arts projects, and field trips.
— Marginal notes are inserted into activities as appropriate, to alert teachers to areas of special sensitivity and to provide examples of the experiences of teachers who class tested the activity.

The appendix includes two sections: (1) Black Line Masters which provide additional information, questionnaires and model letters recommended for use in selected activities and (2) a broad-ranging annotated resource list which describes: fiction and non-fiction books; charts, games and kits; films and videos; filmstrips and audio cassettes; reference books and other publications. Items are categorized according to student (S) and/or teacher (T) use.

General Tips

1. Begin by sending a letter home, informing parents of the nature of the multicultural program, explaining what their children will be doing, and letting them know that you will be needing their involvement. Black Line Master #1 provides an example of this kind of letter. Keep parents informed of developments as the year progresses, through letters, phone calls and the involvement of the parent-teacher school association or its equivalent.

2. Bring awareness of the reality of our multicultural heritage to life by creating a fully multicultural environment, both within the classroom and the school. Try some of the following strategies.
  (i) Encourage school boards and committees to establish multicultural guidelines and policies to ensure that curricula and teaching practices reflect cultural and racial diversity.

(ii) Make sure that the school calendar reflects dates of importance to all cultural and religious groups, especially those represented in your school community. Arrange appropriate celebrations for those dates.

(iii) Ensure that posters, pictures, and artifacts displayed on school walls and in show cases reflect the multicultural fact of our society.

(iv) Stock the classroom and resource centre with books and audio-visual materials which reflect the range of cultural heritages.

(v) Find ways to integrate multiculturalism into music, physical education, current events and other subject areas.

(vi) Organize lunch programs that go beyond the usual "hot dog days". Introduce foods such as East Indian samosas, East European perogies, Chinese egg rolls and the like.

3. Strengthen your own resources by:
   (i) keeping an updated list of parents and others who have helped or expressed willingness to do so;
   (ii) developing an outreach program to key ethno-cultural community groups and individuals who can contribute to school and extra-curricular activities;
   (iii) requesting that the school board Resource Centre develop a multi-media, multicultural section, including multicultural media kits, posters, books, films and periodicals for use in classroom activities.

4. Broaden your own knowledge by keeping abreast of ethno-cultural festivals and celebrations through newspapers and community publications. Try to attend to gain experience, generate ideas, and make contacts.

5. Establish an atmosphere of acceptance by:
   (i) setting a personal example by your own responses to students and colleagues;
   (ii) expecting positive and accepting behaviour from students both in the classroom and school yard.

Glossary

Culture The total way of life of particular groups of people. It includes everything that a group of people thinks, says, does and makes; its customs, language, material artifacts, and shared system of values, beliefs, attitudes and behaviours. Culture is learned and transmitted from generation to generation.

Discrimination An often unfair difference in the treatment of persons, ideas or things.

Equality Having equal access to all that a society affords, regardless of colour, religion, gender, class, ethno-cultural background or other factors.

Ethnic/Ethno-cultural An adjective used to describe a group which shares a common language, origin, heritage or ancestry.

Human Rights The equal right of every person to make for him/herself the life that he/she wishes to have, consistent with his/her duties and obligations as a member of society, without being hindered in or prevented from doing so by discriminatory practices. (adapted from the *Canadian Human Rights Act. Section 2*)

Immigrant A person who has been lawfully permitted to come to Canada to establish permanent residence.

Multiculturalism A policy based on the conviction that people of various cultures who make up Canada can live and interact with one another in a spirit of mutual respect and intercultural understanding, with equal rights and opportunities.

Multiculturalism in Education School programs which help students to understand and take pride in their own heritage and identity and to understand and accept the heritage and identity of others and which promote equality, justice and fairness for all groups.

Prejudice An opinion, often unfavourable, formed without a fair examination of the facts.

Racism A form of prejudice which leads to discrimination against individuals or groups based on their colour or ethnic origin.

Stereotype An oversimplified, often false, mental picture or preconceived view of a particular person, idea, or thing.

Social Studies and Multiculturalism

Social studies curriculum focuses on the study of people and their interactions with others and the environment. The content of social studies comes from the whole range of social sciences, the subjects which examine people and the world, past and present. These include economics, geography, history, political science, as well as sociology, anthropology, environmental studies, current events, and career education.

Social studies transmits much more than knowledge. The values and attitudes of our society are explored, and the skills necessary to live within that society are developed. As students progress through school, their understanding of the social and cultural values of their community, province, and country increases. Social studies ultimately promotes a sense of belonging, socially and culturally, within our democratic system, and fosters an appreciation of individual and collective cultural heritage.

Many of the fundamental aims of social studies curriculum can be achieved using a multicultural approach. These include enabling students to:

— develop an awareness of self and community;
— explore the world through their own experiences;
— develop an awareness of the geographical, historical and cultural realities of Canada and the world;
— take an active part in society;
— develop an understanding of and respect for different cultural values in the community and beyond.

Two themes have been chosen through which to integrate multiculturalism into the social studies curriculum. These themes, along with the activities which develop them, follow.

☐ Canada's Many Cultures
  Activity #1 — Who Am I?
  Activity #2 — Our Needs, Our Cultures
  Activity #3 — Our Origins, Our Backgrounds, Our Family Trees
  Activity #4 — Family Ties
  Activity #5 — Our Places of Origin

☐ Building Our Multicultural Nation
  Activity #6 — The Sum of Our Parts
  Activity #7 — Join Us and Share
  Activity #8 — Why Immigrate? Who is an Immigrant? What is it Like?
  Activity #9 — Tracing Our Time Lines, Discovering Our Roots

Who am I?

Throughout your examination of multiculturalism within social studies, make certain that your students recognize the unique place of aboriginal peoples in the Canadian mosaic. The aboriginal peoples were the first to come to Canada and hold a special place as the ''First People.'' Their experiences should not be confused with those of the settlers and immigrants who followed.

Not all students will identify strongly with an ethnic group. Some may have roots in several groups. There are a number of strategies you can use to deal with these situations. You may ask students to research all groups with which they have links. On the other hand, they can focus on one which they prefer. Some students might be directed to work on groups which are not represented in the class, to provide a broader picture of Canada's multicultural nature. Multiculturalism in Canada: A Graphic Overview is an excellent resource in such situations.

MULTICULTURAL OBJECTIVES

Students should be able to:
— identify and understand characteristics shared by all people;
— increase their self awareness through understanding their heritage;
— develop an awareness of themselves as individuals belonging to an ethno-cultural group(s);
— name some of the ethno-cultural groups which make up our multicultural society;
— become aware of the variety of experiences, lifestyles, beliefs, and activities of various ethno-cultural communities.

SKILL OBJECTIVES

Students should be able to:
— participate in dialogues;
— classify information;
— analyze information.

RESOURCES

— Black Line Master #2

PROCEDURES

☐ Have students write short personal profiles. These should include physical features, likes and dislikes and ethno-cultural background. Students should not sign their names to their profiles.

☐ Collect the profiles and hand them out at random to the class. Have students read the profile they have received aloud in class. Ask the class to guess the identities of the people described.

☐ Have each student fill in the questionnaire on Black Line Master #2. Students should read their replies out loud, leading to a class discussion and exchange on their respective backgrounds.

☐ Ensure that discussion focuses both on what cultures have in common as well as on the varieties in lifestyles, family history, areas of interest and so on within our multicultural society. Students should also understand that people balance their concern with elements of their cultural heritage with those of day to day living.

Our Needs, Our Cultures

This activity helps students identify shared characteristics, before examining their own cultural identities. It is very important that the atmosphere within the classroom is one which models acceptance of different cultures, and ways of living. Students should recognize that all cultures have value and that none is inherently superior or inferior to another.

MULTICULTURAL OBJECTIVES

Students should be able to:
— understand that all people share common needs;
— understand that people meet their needs in similar and different ways, depending on their cultural heritage and personal preferences.

SKILL OBJECTIVES

Students should be able to:
— classify information;
— summarize information.

RESOURCES

— foods from various cultures, including fresh fruits, home cooking and canned goods
— cookbooks with recipes from different cultures

PROCEDURES

☐ Ask students to think about what is basic to all of us for our daily existence and survival. You might ask them to imagine being shipwrecked on a remote island. What would they need to survive?

☐ Write the students' examples on the board. Explain that human needs can be organized into various categories. Give students an opportunity to come up with categories. Develop a list of 8-10, such as the following: 1. food; 2. clothing; 3. shelter; 4. love; 5. communication; 6. membership in a group; 7. beliefs to explain our existence; 8. recreation/entertainment.

☐ Choose a straight forward need, such as food or shelter, and ask students to provide examples of it, listing them on the board under the category.

☐ Divide the class into groups, with a recorder in each, and assign them one need category. Make sure that the groups assigned the more abstract needs, such as the need for a belief to explain our existence, fully understand what these mean. Have each group come up with examples of their need and share these with the class. Write the examples for each need category on the board.

☐ Have the class go into detail about the first human need, food. Ask questions such as the following:
  — Why is food a universal need?
  — What is your favourite food?
  — Where did your favourite food originate?
  — What criteria do you use when you choose the foods you like to eat?
  — Give examples of foods that some people are unable to eat and explain why?

— What are some of the ways that foods are different? (e.g. taste, smell, appearance, nutrients)
— Give examples of foods that are commonly eaten in some other countries and suggest why each is eaten.

☐ Ask students to summarize what they have learned and draw some conclusions about the common need for food. These might include: families pass on eating traditions; many "Canadian" foods originated in other lands; food preferences can be determined by our cultural and/or religious background and so on.

☐ Have your class experience multiculturalism through their palates. List different food categories such as soup, salad, vegetable, bread, potatoes, noodles, meat, fish, dessert, drink on the board. Assign students to bring items from different categories for a multicultural pot luck lunch. The foods that they bring should be items which are popular in their cultural group.

☐ If the cultural diversity in your classroom is limited, bring in a variety of fruits and canned goods from various cultures to share with students. You might also arrange a field trip to a grocery store where the class can discover these foods on the shelves.

☐ Ask students to collect recipes which reflect their ethno-cultural backgrounds and compile these into a multicultural cookbook.

ACTIVITY #3

Our Origins, Our Backgrounds, Our Family Trees

This activity will require sensitivity to different family situations. Some students may be adopted, perhaps cross culturally, and will have no knowledge of their birth parents. Others may be living in single parent, extended, blended or foster families. In some families, parents do not have a lot of information or may be unwilling to share their family experiences publicly. You may also encounter situations where a student's family immigrated from one country, but their ethno-cultural heritage is that of another.

MULTICULTURAL OBJECTIVES

Students should be able to:
— recognize their ethno-cultural identity and roots;
— trace their family origins;
— identify elements of their cultural heritage;
— demonstrate sensitivity to cultural similarities and differences;
— respect and accept the value, dignity, and worth of individuals and groups other than their own.

SKILL OBJECTIVES

Students should be able to:
— prepare and ask interview questions;
— fill in a family tree graphic.

RESOURCES
— Black Line Master #3

PROCEDURES

☐ Have students trace their ancestry through interviews with parents and/or family members. Help them to prepare questions which focus on family origins, such as: Where did our family come from? How many generations have lived in Canada? In which parts of Canada do my relatives live?

□ Provide students with copies of the family tree (Black Line Master #3) and work through a model for the class. Have students complete their family trees, adding aunts, uncles and cousins, if they wish.

□ Ask students to present their family origins to the class, using their family tree, a collection of family photographs, an oral report or a combination of these and/or other methods.

EXTENDED ACTIVITY #3

An eleven year old boy of Chinese origin refused to have anything to do with his grandparents. They lived in Chinatown, and spoke no English. For him, they represented poor Chinese people and he had disassociated himself from them since he was five years old. His teacher was not aware of the situation. When students were tracing their origins through the course of the social studies activities, she asked them to interview older family members, preferably grandparents. The boy asked if this was really necessary and was told that if he had grandparents, he should interview them. He telephoned his grandparents and found himself faced with a difficult task. His grandfather had many anecdotes for each question but he did not speak English, so it was necessary for questions and answers to be translated into and from Cantonese. The boy asked his father for help. The father drove him over to visit his grandparents on four consecutive weekends. Later, the father called the teacher to express his gratitude to the school for helping to bring the family together and strengthen family ties.

RESOURCES
— cardboard, scissors, string

PROCEDURES

□ Bring in pictures of common symbols (for example, symbols for handicapped parking, a railway crossing, peace). Have students identify what each one signifies. Discuss the importance of symbols in our society, using questions like the following:
  — What is a symbol?
  — What are some examples of symbols?
  — Why are symbols important?
  — Do families and individuals also have special objects of significance which symbolize important elements in their lives?
  — What are some family or personal symbols?

□ Ask students to pick an especially meaningful object that is related to their place of origin or culture and another object that is related to their family and home life. Here are some examples: an Easter egg and a pair of skates for a child of Ukrainian heritage with a passion for hockey; a shamrock and a canoe for a child of Irish descent whose family enjoys wilderness adventures; an origami paper folding and a pen for a Japanese Canadian child whose parents are writers; a Canadian flag and an advertisement for a child who is proud of her citizenship and whose family runs a store. Have children draw pictures or make models of their symbols.

□ Next, select students to construct a class family tree. They should cut heavy pieces of cardboard into two large, identical tree shapes. One shape should be slit halfway down from the top and the other slit halfway up from the bottom, so that the two notches can be fitted together into a tree form.

□ Students now can hang their symbols on the tree. This activity can be done over several periods, or extended over a longer time frame. If the latter course is chosen, students can put new objects on the tree as they learn more about their origins, family or cultural group.

Social Studies and Language Arts

PROCEDURES

A. Multicultural Project

☐ One teacher combined activities on family trees with aspects of the biography project described in Activity #14 and had her class work on a major multicultural project. After students had traced their family origins back as far as they could, she had them draw a family tree which would be used as the cover for their project.

☐ She then had students develop questions, based on suggestions in Activity #14 and use them to interview parents and/or grandparents. Questions included the following:

— What was difficult to leave behind when you came to Canada?

— What were your first impressions of Canada?

— What were some of the things you liked about Canada? What were some of the things you didn't like?

— In what ways was Canada the same as your original homeland? In what ways was Canada different?

— Would I have to return to your original homeland to find my roots? Why or why not?

— Did you bring with you a special value, learned in your original homeland, that you would like to pass on to me? If so, what is it?

☐ Students taped their interviews and included both the tape and a written summary of their interviews as part of their project. They also created collages made up of family photographs and magazine clippings.

☐ Had there been aboriginal students in her class, the teacher could have asked them to undertake a study of their communities either now or in the days before and/or soon after European contact.

B. Time Capsule Project

☐ After students have learned about themselves and their families through family trees, autobiographies and so on, ask them to create a time capsule which would be opened 200 years from now. They should each bring in one object which tells a lot about their culture and/or themselves, and attach to it a short note explaining why the object is so significant.

Family Ties

This activity requires special sensitivity. Because of our material wealth, some immigrant children may compare their country of origin unfavourably to Canada. Others might make the same kinds of negative comparisons between city and country life. Try to guide the class discussion to focus on positive elements. One technique is to have children name two good things and one bad thing about a situation.

You may also find that for some refugee children, discussion about family members in their homeland is very painful. They may not know where relatives are, or even if they are alive. Listen carefully to these children and help them to share those experiences that they feel comfortable talking about, in a format that is best suited to their needs, and respects their feelings.

MULTICULTURAL OBJECTIVES

Students should be able to:
— understand and appreciate their place of origin and family heritage;
— demonstrate knowledge about other parts of Canada and the world;
— learn more about their family history;
— become aware of the personal links that class members have with other parts of Canada and the world.

SKILL OBJECTIVES

Students should be able to:
— write letters;
— ask and answer questions;
— locate geographic areas.

RESOURCES

— stationary, stamps

PROCEDURES

☐ Ask students if they have family members living in another town or city, another part of Canada, or another part of the world. Use class discussion to answer questions like the following:
  — What is the name of the place where your relatives live?
  — Did your family originate in that place, or did the relative move to it from their place of origin? If the relative moved there, why?
  — Have you ever visited this relative? If so, what was the town/city like and how did it compare with your home town/city? Criteria might include size, climate, industries, recreational facilities, languages spoken.
  — Have family members living far away visited with you? If so, what were their reactions to your home town/city? Way of life?

☐ Have students write to a relative in a distant place, asking for information about their lives. If there are students who do not have a relative to write to, pair them with others who do.

☐ To help students get started, brainstorm possible topics for questions. These could include: the type of area they live in: city, suburb, town, village; their family: members, ages, occupations; what they like to do in their leisure time; what they like most about where they live. Students could request that the family member include a postcard and/or pictures with their reply.

☐ Students could present what they have discovered about life in a different place in the form of a display, a composition, or an oral report to the class.

☐ Review what students have discovered, highlighting similarities and differences and emphasizing the value of the network of contacts and experiences they have gained.

ACTIVITY #5

Our Places of Origin

Students should have some experience with map work before getting involved in this activity. There is an overlap with the previous activity, but here the focus is more on awareness of geographic facts rather than on personal experience.

MULTICULTURAL OBJECTIVES

Students should be able to:
— understand the geographic relationship between where they live and where their family originated;
— compare the physical features of where they live with those of the place(s) where their family originated;
— develop awareness of where they live in relation to the rest of Canada and in relation to the rest of the world;

SKILL OBJECTIVES

Students should be able to:
— locate places on maps;
— compare and contrast geographic areas;
— deal effectively with the spatial concepts of size, shape and distance.

RESOURCES
— blank maps of Canada and the world
— globe
— atlas

PROCEDURES

☐ Provide students with two maps, one of Canada and one of the world. Work together as a class, leading the students as they fill in details on one of the maps about the place(s) of origin of their family. (You may have to provide special maps for students working on smaller countries or provinces.) Using an atlas and/or globe, students should fill in geographic details such as: name of country and main cities, names of major bodies of water, details of the topography.

☐ Once the maps are filled in, students can use the atlas to discover details about population, climate, farming, industry, trade and other topics of interest. This information should be written in student notebooks.

☐ Working in groups, students should draw up comparisons between different countries of origin, using criteria such as size, population, major cities and towns, climate, economy.

The Sum of Our Parts

MULTICULTURAL OBJECTIVES

Students should be able to:
— name different ethnic groups living in their province and country;
— describe the size of their ethnic group within the province and country;
— see their class and local community within the context of a multicultural Canadian society.

SKILL OBJECTIVES

Students should be able to:
— use and construct charts and graphs;
— make comparisons;
— research and understand statistical data.

RESOURCES

— Bowers, Vivien and Diane Swanson. *Exploring Canada: Learning from the Past, Looking to the Future*
— *The Canadian Encyclopedia* (Volumes I-IV)
— *Multiculturalism in Canada. A Graphic Overview*
— Statistical information on demographics from provincial government sources
— Black Line Masters #4, #5, #6, #7, #8, #9

PROCEDURES

☐ Begin this activity by asking questions like the following:
   — What can we say about the cultural origins of the people in this classroom?
   — How do you think the cultural make-up of the classroom compares with that of the rest of the school? the community: the province? Canada?
☐ Have students develop graphs which illustrate the ethno-cultural make up of the classroom.
☐ Provide students with government of Canada statistics on multiculturalism. Black Line Masters #4, #5, #6, #7, #8, and #9 can be used. You may also get statistical information from municipal and provincial governments. Have students discover how many people from their cultural group live in the province and in Canada. Display the information on the board and ask students to make observations from the data. For example, how the cultural diversity within the classroom is similar to, or different from that of (a) the province and (b) the country.

Join Us and Share

MULTICULTURAL OBJECTIVES

Students should be able to:

— understand that many ideas and values are universal and have their origins far back in time;

— learn about other cultures from oral presentations;

— recognize that personal stories are the building blocks of history.

SKILL OBJECTIVES

Students should be able to:

— write letters of invitation and thanks;

— listen for details;

— ask questions after an oral presentation;

— solve problems creatively.

RESOURCES

— paper for invitation and thank you notes

— tape recorder and/or video camera (optional)

— refreshments

PROCEDURES

☐ Find out from students if they have grandparents or other family members who might come to class to share their history with the class. After students have checked at home, compile a tentative list of guests, assign dates, and ask students to write to their relative, inviting them to class. Try to ensure a balance between immigrants and those who were born in Canada.

☐ Discuss creative ways to allow those who are not comfortable giving a formal presentation in English to participate. These might include students acting as interpreters, using photographs or objects, or having the guest demonstrate a game or a skill.

☐ Phone each of the invited guests to find out details of their ethno-cultural background and language capabilities. Discuss some strategies and techniques they might use in their presentations. Go over some of the topics which should be included, such as: their childhood and family way of life; where they grew up and what it was like; some interesting experiences; why, if they immigrated, they left their homeland and why they or their family chose Canada.

☐ Before each visitor arrives, locate their country or place of origin on a map. Discuss its relationship to Canada in terms of size and distance.

☐ Have the student briefly introduce the family member. If possible, tape or video record the presentation (with the visitor's permission, of course)

☐ After the visitor has presented his/her information, have students ask questions. Either the teacher or a student should then thank the guest on behalf of the class and refreshments should be served.

☐ Collect the names, addresses and phone numbers of each visitor for your inventory of neighbourhood resources for future activities.

☐ Write a class note to each guest, thanking him/her for their presentation, and noting what was learned from the visit.

☐ Have follow-up discussion about what students have learned about universal values and experiences from the visitors.

Why Immigrate? Who is an Immigrant? What is it Like?

This activity touches another potentially sensitive issue — why people immigrate. The process may have been painful for the families of your students and they may not wish to discuss it in class.

MULTICULTURAL OBJECTIVES

Students should be able to:
— empathize with the experiences of immigrants;
— describe both achievements and problems of immigrants now and in the past;
— understand more about their province, its people, and its possible appeal to new arrivals.

SKILL OBJECTIVES

Students should be able to:
— interview people about their experiences;
— draw conclusions from data;
— solve problems creatively;
— express an idea using a creative mode, such as poetry, poster, letter, booklet, collage.

RESOURCES

— parents, family, neighbours, friends
— Bowers, Vivien and Diane Swanson. *Exploring Canada. Learning from the Past, Looking to the Future*
— Kurelek, William and Margaret S. Engelhart. *They Sought A New World! The Story of European Immigration to North America*
— *Strangers at the Door.* (Film)
— Black Line Masters #10, #11, and #12

PROCEDURES

☐ Begin with a class discussion, posing general questions such as the following:
　　— Is there anyone in the class (or in Canada) who does not have an immigrant among their ancestors?
　　— Why would people leave their countries of origin? Why would they choose to come to Canada?

☐ Ask students to gather some first hand experiences of immigra-

A grade four teacher developed a survey sheet for parents, asking them why they or their family had immigrated and the year they had arrived in Canada. She then drew a large time line on a piece of construction paper, and had students write their family's immigration history on it. The primary place of the aboriginal people was recognized. This activity promoted a strong sense of pride in ancestry among the children.

tion by interviewing family, friends and/or neighbours with memories of immigration to Canada. Students should find out why they left their countries of origin and what they experienced when they arrived in Canada. The latter might include memories of both positive and negative episodes.

☐ Use the information which students collect to make a chart on the board. Classify each reason for immigrating by country of origin and year. You might divide the reasons into the "push" factors such as poverty, discrimination, war or unrest which caused people to leave their homelands and the "pull" features like jobs, peace, democracy, opportunities, and established family, which attracted immigrants to Canada. As you discuss why people immigrate, note the variety of reasons within ethno-cultural groups. Examine patterns of immigration for individual groups and consider possible explanations for increases and declines in numbers.

☐ Divide the class into groups to discuss either 1) the features of your province (or of Canada) which attracted immigrants in the past, as well as some of the difficulties they faced and reasons for the difficulties or 2) the features of your province (or of Canada) which attract immigrants today and some of the difficulties that newcomers might face.

☐ As a class, read Black Line Master #10, "Making a New Life". Discuss individual case stories, relating them to the information that students acquired in their own interviews when appropriate. Again, make sure that students recognize different experiences within given ethno-cultural groups, in order to avoid stereotyping and to explain different reasons for immigrating to Canada.

☐ After completing the case stories, ask students to do the following:
   — List all of the things that they would have to give up if they were immigrating to another country.
   — Imagine how they would feel about moving away from relatives and friends.
   — Think of ways to solve some of the problems described in the stories. Have them role play some of the situations to show their solutions.

☐ Select a book such as *They Sought A New World* to read to the class or for students to read on their own. Alternatively, view the film *Strangers at the Door*. These provide insights into immigrant experiences. Students could write a review of the book or film, draw a book cover or an advertisement for the film, role play a key scene or present an oral report.

☐ Introduce students to Black Line Master #11, "I'd Like to be an Immigrant", a letter written by a young Jamaican girl. After students have read the letter, ask questions like the following:
   — Where do you think Annette got her images or ideas of Canada? Do you think these images are correct? Why or why not?

- If Annette visited Canada, which images and ideas might change? Which might stay the same?
- Describe some new experiences for Annette if she were to visit Canada (a) in winter? in spring? in summer? in fall? (b) if she visited a large city? a town or village? a farm? a ranch?
- Which of the following might be new experiences for you if you visited Jamaica: climate? geography? people? language(s)? schools? food? holidays? sports?
- Where could you find out more about Jamaica and Jamaicans before leaving Canada?

☐ Have students read the poem "My Home, My Home", Black Line Master #12. Ask them to compare their own (or their family's) feelings with those of I-Syin.

☐ Ask students to choose one of the following projects to promote immigration to their province:
- Write a poem about the province and its people
- Design a poster advertising the appeal of the province
- Put together a booklet containing a profile of the province and its people
- Make a collage of magazine pictures and newspaper headlines reflecting the image of the province. Make sure that the collage shows the province's ethno-cultural make up.

EXTENDED ACTIVITY #8

RESOURCES
- Black Line Master #13

PROCEDURES
☐ Have students "become" an immigrant and write a log describing their journey to and early days in Canada. Information could come from interviews conducted earlier, or the log could describe the imagined experiences of a new immigrant.

☐ Provide students with the list of topics on Black Line Master #13 to guide them as they write.

☐ When logs have been checked and corrected, collate them into a booklet which can be shared by the class.

Tracing Our Time Lines, Discovering Our Roots

MULTICULTURAL OBJECTIVES

Students should be able to:

— appreciate the unique place of the aboriginal peoples in Canadian history;
— recognise that, with the exception of aboriginal peoples, all Canadians are immigrants or the descendants of immigrants;
— appreciate the cultural diversity of their community and country;
— develop an historical perspective on their own origins and that of the community.

SKILL OBJECTIVES

Students should be able to:

— plot time lines;
— find information in reference books;

RESOURCES

— *Canada's Ethnic Groups Series*
— *The Canadian Encyclopedia* (Volumes I-IV)
— Conner, Daniel C.G. and Doreen Bethune Johnson. *Native People and Explorers of Canada*

PROCEDURES

☐ Provide students with reference materials and have them work in groups, exploring the migration and settlement patterns of the aboriginal peoples in the province or of one aboriginal group in the area. Groups should then share their information with the class.

☐ Direct students to the reference materials which describe the growth of ethno-cultural groups within Canada. Have students prepare a time line, showing the growth of their group. Then ask students to prepare a family time line, noting the key dates when family members came to Canada. Alternatively, students could produce one time line, using different colours to indicate group and family highlights.

☐ Compare time lines and discuss waves of immigration, as well as how some ethno-cultural groups were welcomed at certain points in time, while others were not. You may have to introduce groups which were not examined in class.

Language Arts and Multiculturalism

Language is a tool we use to communicate with other members of our society. We all use language expressively, when we talk and write, and receptively, when we read or listen. The four interrelated and interdependent skills of speaking, writing, reading and listening are the foundation of language arts programs.

Experience and language grow together. As the world of the child expands, so too does his/her skill and pleasure with language. Language arts programs capitalize on the child's experiences and provide new ones to ensure this growth.

Language is used to establish relationships among our experiences and to organize and refine our ideas. In this way, language is a vehicle for thinking, as well as being a stimulus for thinking.

The multicultural strategies developed in this unit will help teachers meet many of the goals inherent in language arts programs, including enabling students to:

— formulate ideas clearly;
— develop a precise, varied, appropriate vocabulary;
— organize ideas logically, clearly and interestingly;
— use language that is appropriate to the audience;
— select the appropriate forms for written and oral communication;
— understand and interpret the meaning of words;
— appreciate the literature of different cultures.

The themes selected for this unit expand outward from the individual to society and the world. Literature, ranging from biography to folk tales, is drawn from different cultures and lifestlyes.

☐ Names
   Activity #10 — Introducing Ourselves
   Activity #11 — Our Names
   Activity #12 — How our Names are Chosen

☐ Autobiography/Biography
   Activity #13 — My Autobiography
   Activity #14 — Our Neighbourhood

☐ Children in Fiction
   Activity #15 — Families
   Activity #16 — Feeling Different
   Activity #17 — How we can Help
   Activity #18 — Discrimination

Activity #19 — New Canadians

☐ Folk Tales, Fables, Fairy Tales
Activity #20 — Calendars
Activity #21 — Is this Fair? Does Justice Prevail?
Activity #22 — Telling our own Tales

☐ Our World Today
Activity #23 — Justice and Injustice in the News

ACTIVITY #10

Introducing Ourselves

This activity can be used as an "ice breaker" at the start of the school year, to help familiarize students with each other's names. It could also be combined with Activity #1.

MULTICULTURAL OBJECTIVES

Students should be able to:
— learn the names of classmates;
— pronounce names correctly.

SKILL OBJECTIVES

Students should be able to:
— articulate clearly;
— follow directions.

RESOURCES

— manilla and construction paper, scissors, glue, pen/pencils

PROCEDURES

☐ Ask students to print their first and last names in capital letters on manilla paper, name tag size. They should then cut out their names, using unusual shapes (e.g. hearts, hexagons) if they wish, and glue them to a piece of coloured construction paper. You should do the same with your name.

☐ Collect the name tags and place them in a box. Have students take turns drawing a name tag from the box and pronouncing it correctly. The child (or teacher) whose name is picked will determine if the pronounciation is correct. The whole class should then repeat the name in unison.

ACTIVITY #11

Our Names

MULTICULTURAL OBJECTIVES

Students should be able to:
— become familiar with different names from various cultures;
— describe the meaning/history of their first and last/family names.

SKILL OBJECTIVES

Students should be able to:
— research the origin of names.

RESOURCES

— class list
— Browder, Sue. *The New Age Baby Book*
— *Black Line Masters #14, #15*

PROCEDURES

☐ Read Black Line Master #14, ''Names Can be Similar But Different'', to the class. Use the questions on the sheet to generate interest in the wide variety of first and last family names and their roots.

☐ Alternatively, read from *The New Age Baby Book* or a similar reference about how various cultures choose names for their children.

☐ Use questions like the following as the basis for a class discussion:

  — Are there any people in your class, school or community who share your family name but are not related to you?
  — Do you know how a common name, such as John, is spelt and pronounced in some other languages?
  — Does your family name (or that of a friend) have a meaning? If so, what is it and how do you think it originated?
  — People sometimes change their names by making them shorter, simpler, or altogether different. Why do you think they would do so?

☐ Pass out a class list to students and have them use it to answer the questions on Black Line Master #15.

☐ Have students design a family crest or symbol reflecting what they have discovered about their name.

☐ Ask students who have other language capabilities to translate their class mates' names into different languages.

ACTIVITY #12

How Our Names are Chosen

MULTICULTURAL OBJECTIVES

Students should be able to:
— understand how different cultures and religions choose names for their children;
— recognize that some names have personal as well as cultural/ religious significance;
— understand why some people change their names;
— recognize the values of different beliefs and customs.

SKILL OBJECTIVES

Students should be able to:
— interpret ideas;
— ask questions;
— make oral presentations.

RESOURCES

— Black Line Masters #16, #17
— Browder, Sue. *The New Age Baby Book*
— family records

PROCEDURES

☐ Hand out copies of Black Line Master #16, ''Naming Customs''. Use it as a spring board for a discussion about different naming customs. The following questions can be used as a starting point.
  — Why do some people have one first name, while others have double or middle names?
  — What role does your religion play in selecting the name of a child?
  — Are there any similarities in the ways that different cultural and religious groups name children? If so, what are they?
  — How have naming practices changed over time and in different situations?
  — Has your name ever been altered? When? Why?

☐ Provide students with a copy of Black Line Master #17 and have them go over the questions with their families. The following issues could be raised before or after students share the results of their questionnaire.
  — how historical and other circumstances may have been responsible for changes in family and first names;
  — how the names of aboriginal people have so often been ''translated'';
  — how and why certain names become popular, then lose popularity over time.

☐ You may want to assign groups of students to research the naming practices and history of names in cultures which have not been covered in class.

☐ Ask students what name they would choose (a) for themselves and (b) for their future children and explain their choices.

ACTIVITY #13

My Autobiography

MULTICULTURAL OBJECTIVES

Students should be able to:
— develop and retain a personal cultural identity by learning more about their heritage and developing a sense of continuity with the past;

In the next two activities, children begin to see the class or neighbourhood as reflections of the larger society and to recognize that people's individual stories are what make up our multicultural country.

— share personal and cultural experiences;
— recognize that everyone is important and has a story to tell.

SKILL OBJECTIVES
Students should be able to:
— understand the structure and content of autobiographies;
— organize ideas into a logical sequence;
— acquire information through interviews;
— write autobiographies;
— give and receive editorial advice.

RESOURCES
— An autobiography with a strong sense of ethno-cultural identity, such as:
    — *Childhood Memories of A Japanese Canadian — Lost Years.* (Filmstrip)
    — Frank, Anne. *Anne Frank. The Diary of a Young Girl*
    — Fritz, Jean. *Homesick. My Own Story*
    — Reiss, Johanna. *The Upstairs Room*
    — Segal, Lore. *Other People's Houses*
    — Takashima, Shizuye. *A Child in a Prison Camp*

PROCEDURES
☐ Read an autobiography to the class over a given period. Each day, ask questions about the content and format which allow students to explore the following:
    — how autobiographies are written;
    — some important incidents which are included in auto-biographies;
    — elements of autobiographies which make them interesting/enjoyable.
  Write their answers on the board for future reference.
☐ When you have finished reading the autobiography, ask students to suggest topics which should be covered in writing an auto-biography.
    These might include:
    — background — ancestors, birthplace, culture;
    — beginnings — anecdotes of parents and relatives about earliest years;
    — earliest memories — happy, sad, surprising, unusual incidents;
    — special events — birthdays, holidays, celebrations;
    — important people — family, friends, teachers.
☐ Once students have made a list of topics, they can begin research-ing their own autobiographies. Discuss how cultural heritage or individual and family experiences will be reflected in what they write. Suggest that they ask parents and grandparents to describe incidents and anecdotes of their babyhood and early childhood. Assign a date for completion of chapter one.
☐ Divide the class into small groups and have students read their

chapters aloud to the group. Group members should ask themselves whether they can follow the story and whether or not the story is interesting, then provide the writer with feedback and suggestions for improvements in the areas of content, structure and style.

☐ The writer should then describe his/her plans for the next chapter and get group advice concerning content and structure. Have students follow this procedure until they have completed their autobiographies.

☐ During the course of this activity, circulate among the groups, helping with individual or group problems and checking that students are "on the right track". You may also bring the class together several times, to discuss the procedure and share experiences.

☐ When students have written their autobiographies, have them add illustrations and/or photographs. The completed autobiographies can be combined into a class book and circulated within the class and/or school.

ACTIVITY #14

Our Neighbourhood

Be careful to ensure that discussions do not lead to "blaming the victim". It is the responses of other people to cultural, religious, gender and/or other differences which cause problems, rather than the differences themselves.

MULTICULTURAL OBJECTIVES

Students should be able to:
— understand and appreciate the experiences of people with given cultural origins;
— understand and appreciate how peoples' cultural backgrounds influence their lives;
— describe the ethno-cultural make up of their neighbourhood.

SKILL OBJECTIVES

Students should be able to:
— develop questionnaires;
— interview people;
— select relevant information;
— interpret, verify and edit material.

RESOURCES

— A biography with a strong sense of ethno-cultural identity, such as:
  — Bull, Angela. *Anne Frank — Profiles*
  — Coerr, Eleanor. *Sedako and the Thousand Cranes*
  — Greenwood, Barbara and Audrey McKim. *Her Special Vision*
  — Petry, Ann. *Harriet Tubman, Conductor of the Underground Railway*
  — Sawyer, Don. *Where the Rivers Meet*
  — Sterling, Dorothy. *Freedom Train*

Prepare students for their interviews by emphasizing the need to be sensitive to their subjects' feelings. People are often shy about being questioned, or may belong to cultures which consider these kinds of questions rude. Students themselves might not feel comfortable approaching "strangers". In that case, you will have to make some initial contacts in the community or develop strategies to help students overcome their reluctance. A final caution: guard against stereotyping by reminding students that the experience and/or life style of an individual does not represent those of the whole community.

— people in the neighbourhood
— tape/video recorder (optional)

PROCEDURES

☐ Choose one biography and read it to the class. Have questions like the following written on the board before you begin reading, so students can think about content and format while they listen to the biography.

Sample Questions — CONTENT
— At what point in the biography do we learn of the person's family background?
— How does the main character's background (culture, religion, colour, socio-economic level) influence how he or she chooses to live?
— How do other people react to the main character? In what ways do the attitudes of others to the main character's family background influence his or her life?
— What are some positive and negative experiences which influenced the life of the main character. Describe their impact on his/her life?

Sample Questions — FORMAT
— What were some of the important things that the author had to know about the character before being able to write their biography?
— What are some of the characteristics of a biography?

☐ After finishing the biography, go over the questions with the class, ensuring that they understand both the content and format of a biography.

☐ Introduce the "Neighbourhood Biography" project, explaining that students will be developing biographies to illustrate the variety of people who live and/or work in their community.

☐ Have students choose partners or team up students in pairs. Ask them to select someone in the neighbourhood (eg. school employee, business person, store owner or employee, medical or dental worker, politician, media personality etc. . .) whose biography they would like to write. They may choose family members if they wish. Teams should introduce and explain their choices to the class. Make sure that the biographies represent a broad look at the community.

☐ Ask teams to make up questions for interviewing the person they have chosen. Emphasize that their questions should focus both on the person's current situation (for example their job, interests, family life) and on their past.

☐ Compile a class list of questions on the board, and have teams add to their own list any others that would improve their interviews. Remind students that personal anecdotes will add interest and colour to their biographies.

☐ You may want to add items from the sample questions below to ensure that students get information on the ethno-cultural background of the people they interview.

Sample questions for all biographies:
— Where did your ancestors come from?
— Do you and your family celebrate festivals and/or holidays that have been part of your family tradition for a long time? What are these and how are they celebrated?
— Can you speak and/or write the language of your ancestors? Can your children speak and/or write this language?
— Can you tell me any stories about your ancestors' lives?
— Did your ancestors pass on any skills to you?

Sample questions for biographies of people who have arrived recently:
— What is your country of origin?
— When did you come to Canada?
— Why did you decide to leave your country of origin? Why did you choose Canada as a new homeland?
— What were some of your first reactions to Canada? Was Canada like you had hoped it would be?
— How has your life changed since coming to Canada?

☐ Have students contact the persons they have chosen and set up an appointment for an interview. Team members should bring a tape or video recorder to the interview if possible, and ask the person whether he or she minds if they record the interview. As one member asks the questions, the other team member listens carefully, writing down answers if the interview is not being taped. Additional questions can be added along the way.

☐ Ask students to bring their tapes or notes to class. Select one or two teams and play their tapes or read their notes to the class. Ask students to consider how the information they have heard can be used to answer the questions about the content and form of biographies discussed earlier. This will help the class select the parts of their interviews which will be most effective in writing up their biographies.

☐ Once students understand how to use the materials they have gathered, ask them to write their biographies, using illustrations as appropriate. Compile all of them into a class book titled "Our Neighbourhood".

☐ Ensure that students write thank you notes to the people who they interviewed. If possible, make a copy of "Our Neighbourhood" for each person interviewed as a special "thank you".

EXTENDED ACTIVITY #14
_____

PROCEDURES
☐ Cross reference this activity with Activity #6, "The Sum of Our Parts", and compare roughly the ethno-cultural make up of the neighbourhood as identified by the students, with that of the province and the country.

Families

Help students to understand that the concept of family varies from culture to culture. This story deals with an extended family. Other types of families should be explored in class discussion. Be sensitive to the need for acceptance of a wide range of situations within families, including varying roles of women, children and elders.

Students might conclude that some cultural groups do not look after their elderly, while others do. Deal with this reverse stereotype as you would with any stereotype, pointing out the dangers of overgeneralizations.

MULTICULTURAL OBJECTIVES

Students should be able to:
— understand lifestyles that are different from their own;
— appreciate that the roles of family members can be determined by cultural traditions;
— understand relationships within families that are different from and similar to those within their own families.

SKILL OBJECTIVES

Students should be able to:
— make comparisons;
— write a descriptive composition.

RESOURCES

— ''Shonar Arches'' in *Camels Can Make You Homesick* by Nazneen Sadiq, or another story involving a protagonist who lives in an extended family or in other types of families explored in class.

PROCEDURES

☐ Read, or have a student read ''Shonar Arches'' or a similar story to the class. Have questions like the following on the board when the story is read, to focus student's attention on the family unit being depicted.

  Sample Questions about the story:
  — Who are the members of the main character's family?
  — Is any family member particularly important? If so, how can you tell?
  — Do family roles and relationships change at any point in the story? If so, how do they change?
  — What is the main character's dilemma within the family?
  — What happens to make him/her come to terms with the dilemma?

  Sample Questions about your family:
  — Does anyone who is not a member of your immediate family (mother, father, brothers and/or sisters) live with you?
  — Who in your family makes the major decisions?
  — What role do your grandparents play in decision making in your family?
  — Compare your family roles and relationships with those of another family you know.

☐ Discuss some of the general similarities and differences between families to help students understand various family structures and styles.

☐ Ask students to write a short descriptive composition, introducing

their family and explaining how it functions. Provide questions like the following to help guide students as they write:
— How many family members live at your house?
— Who are they?
— Do they live with you all year long?
— What role do the women and girls in the family play? the men and boys?
— Do you have grandparents? What are they like? Describe some of your other relatives and the role they play in your family.
— What helps your parents and/or grandparents and/or relatives play their roles within your family?
— What are your responsibilities within the family to (a) your parents (b) your grandparents (c) other relatives

☐ Collect the compositions and select several to compare on the board, using criteria such as: family members at home; role of family members; responsibilities of family members. After completing the comparison, ask students to write a sentence summarizing the positive features of a family lifestyle that is not their own.

EXTENDED ACTIVITY #15

PROCEDURES

A. Field Trip 1

Arrange for students to visit a Senior Citizens' Centre. Where possible, contact centres run by ethno-cultural communities. Work with the centre to pair up each student with an "adoptive grandparent". Explain that students will be asking questions about the senior citizen's family life, so that they can develop an understanding of different family lifestyles. Have students prepare their questions before the visit, and remind them that they should be prepared to adapt their questions to suit the person and situation as necessary. You might invite some or all of the "adoptees" to address the classes and share their experience.

B. Field Trip 2

Pair students with different types of families and have the partners learn about one another's family. Partners should visit each other's homes, perhaps for dinner, to observe and participate in a family way of life different from their own. Students should consider the advantages of the different life style, then write a paragraph describing their observations.

☐ In both of the above situations, discuss the extent to which the family lifestyles they have learned about/observed reflect a cultural heritage and/or an individual situation. Help students avoid easy generalizations as they experience and learn about various family lifestyles in a changing multicultural society.

Feeling Different

Remind students that while cultural differences often enrich our society, people do not always respond positively to these differences.

MULTICULTURAL OBJECTIVES

Students should be able to:
— understand and appreciate cultural differences and how they enrich a multicultural society;
— empathize with people who are having difficulties dealing with their ethno-cultural identities within the larger society;

SKILL OBJECTIVES

Students should be able to:
— make comparisons;
— observe patterns in information;
— interpret stories;
— research information;
— write a story.

RESOURCES

— "The Muslin Curtains" in *The Dancing Sun*, Jan Andrews (editor), or a similar story in which the protagonist is made to feel like an outsider by peers and is ashamed of his/her family as a result.
— "Peacocks and Bandaids" in *Camels Can Make You Homesick*, by Nazneen Sadiq, or a similar story in which the main character is afraid to display skills and talents gained through his/her heritage, for fear of ridicule.

PROCEDURES

☐ Before introducing students to the stories, discuss the concept of "feeling different". You may want to start with the discussion questions which follow and expand upon them as appropriate.
— Have you ever felt different from your peers?
— If so, why did you feel different? (for example, because of your religion, skin colour, clothing, height, weight)
— What was it like to feel different?
— Did feeling different come from inside or was it a response to the reaction of your peers?
— How did you deal with your peers in these situations?
— What would the rest of the class do if confronted with some of these situations?
— Have you ever tried to make someone else feel different? If so, why?
— What does "different" mean? Is it just a negative word, or can it be positive too?
— Would you like to live in a world where we were all the same? Why or why not?
— What might happen to the way we look at ourselves and others if we used the word "unique" instead of "different"?

One teacher asked her class to write ''prejudice/discrimination'' instead of ''feeling different'' stories. By using these as case studies, she demonstrated the relationship between this activity and the issues raised in Activity #30.

☐ Read ''The Muslin Curtains'' or a similar story to the class. Ask students to think about the protagonist's dilemma and put themselves in her place as they listen to the story.

☐ After reading the story, ask the class for their reactions to and feelings about the protagonist, her family and her classmates. Explore the extent to which Merna's classmates were the cause of her difficulties and how they could have acted differently.

☐ Have the class consider whether Merna actually found a solution to her problem. Was it a permanent or temporary solution?

☐ Now read ''Peacocks and Bandaids'' or a similar story. Ask the class to focus on the main character and his (or her) situation and to compare his or her dilemma with that of the protagonist in ''The Muslin Curtains''.

☐ Divide the class into groups, with a recorder assigned to each, and ask them to consider the following questions about the two stories.
   — Compare the ''feeling of being different'' of the main characters in the two stories. How is it the same? different?
   — Compare the relationship that the main characters in each story have with their family and friends. How are they the same? different?
   — What might happen in each of the stories if we substituted ''unique'' for ''different''?

☐ After the groups discuss the questions, the recorder should summarize their answers in a paragraph or on a chart. Groups should then share their answers and discuss similarities and differences in their observations.

☐ Ask the same groups to create a ''feeling different'' story, in which the main character faces similar dilemmas to those in the stories they have studied. These differences need not be related to ethno-cultural heritage. In fact, they should set the issue within the context of their lives. For example, students might explore the world of teenage trends or fashions and being different. These stories could be used as case studies by the class. In conclusion, ask students to once again consider what happens when the word ''different'' is changed to ''unique''.

EXTENDED ACTIVITY #16

PROCEDURES

☐ Both recommended stories deal with dance forms. Have students research dance in various cultures. You may assign cultures to individuals or groups or have students select one on their own. The results of this research can be shared with the class orally or in the form of a bulletin board display.

☐ Students who are able to perform a particular form of dance could be invited to do one for their peers. You may want to contact families or community groups to arrange for dance demonstrations.

ACTIVITY #17

How We Can Help

MULTICULTURAL OBJECTIVES

Students should be able to:
— understand how cultural practices can influence identity;
— understand different cultural identities and practices;
— deal effectively with cultural similarities and differences.

SKILL OBJECTIVES

Students should be able to:
— formulate hypotheses;
— draw conclusions;
— solve problems;
— form value judgments.

RESOURCES

— ''Figs for Everyone'' in *Camels Can Make You Homesick*, by Nazneen Sadiq, or a similar story in which the protagonist is apprehensive about links with traditional ways which result in being teased by peers
— Black Line Master #18

PROCEDURES

☐ Review with the class how people are made to feel different and list them on the board.

☐ Refer back to ''The Muslin Curtain'' or its equivalent. Have students consider why the solution to the main character's problems was not entirely positive. How might they turn it around to achieve a better outcome? Ask them to think of negative ''feeling different'' situations that ended up positively.

☐ Read or have a student read ''Figs for Everyone'' or its equivalent. Use a sequence of questions like those below to help students discover the theme of the story.
   — Why did the main character feel ''different''?
   — Why did the main character feel that friends would not understand his or her customs and behaviours?
   — Can someone be called a friend if they do not understand? Explain your answer?
   — Did anyone understand the main character's feelings? If so, why? How did they show that they understood?
   — What did the understanding person do to help the main character with his or her dilemma?
   — What is the theme of the story?

☐ Hand out Black Line Master #18, ''How We Can Help''. After students have completed the sheet, develop a student code of behaviour, titled ''Do Unto Others'', ''Don't Do Unto Others'', listing student's answers to questions 7 and 8. Display the code on the bulletin board.

PROCEDURES

☐ Invite a Muslim parent or member of the East Indian community to explain the significance of traditional hand painting. They should explain when it is done, why it is done, who does it, the type of paint used and any other aspects which interest students.

☐ Have a student volunteer to be a model and ask your guest to demonstrate the art on his/her hands. Request that the guest use water colours rather than the customary dyes so that the colours will be easier to wash off.

ACTIVITY #18

Discrimination

MULTICULTURALISM OBJECTIVES

Students should be able to:
— understand how discrimination affects both those who discriminate and those who are discriminated against;
— realize that discrimination comes in many forms and must be dealt with;
— encourage pride in one's ancestry.

SKILL OBJECTIVES

Students should be able to:
— hypothesize;
— write case studies.

REFERENCES

— "Teach Me to Fly, Skyfighter" in *Teach Me to Fly, Skyfighter and Other Stories* by Paul Yee, or a similar story in which the main character discriminates against members of his/her own ethno-cultural group
— Black Line Master #19
— *My Name is Susan Yee*. (film) Or a similar film or book which emphasizes pride in one's ancestry

PROCEDURES

☐ Begin by discussing the meaning of discrimination and other related concepts such as stereotypes, prejudice and racism. (see Glossary, pages 8). The following questions can be used:
— Define discrimination in your own words, using examples. (Help students to understand that discrimination takes many forms, including sexism, racism, "ageism" and so on)
— Why do you think people discriminate against others?
— What can we do to overcome the problem of discrimination?

Review the case studies before they are presented to the class to make sure that they do not, themselves, encourage discriminatory attitudes or behaviour.

□ Point out, if this has not been raised in the discussion, that discrimination does not come only from outside a community or group, but can exist between people of the same ethno-cultural background.

□ Read aloud, or have students read the short story "Teach Me to Fly, Skyfighter" or an equivalent. Hand out copies of Black Line Master #19 or similar questions for students to work on individually or in small groups. Discuss the responses among the class.

□ Divide the class into small groups, with a recorder assigned to each. The groups should work together to write a case study describing a situation which they feel illustrates discrimination. The story can be based on a real life experience or be completely imaginary. Have students share their case studies with the class. The class should try to come up with solutions to the problems in each case study.

□ Show the film or an equivalent. Compare it with the story read previously, using criteria such as: main characters; situation; outcomes.

ACTIVITY #19

New Canadians

Your sensitivity towards children who do not see themselves as belonging to any particular ethno-cultural group, or whose families do not practice the customs of their heritage cannot be over emphasised. People are not only free to celebrate or worship and/or practice, but are also free NOT to do so.

MULTICULTURAL OBJECTIVES

Students should be able to:
— empathize with the identity problems faced by newly arrived immigrants;
— appreciate how Canadians with diverse origins retain their cultural traditions and identities.

SKILL OBJECTIVE

Students should be able to:
— express ideas;
— research a topic (Extended Activity)
— display information in chart form (Extended Activity)

RESOURCES

— Tanaka, Shelley. *Michi's New Year*, or a similar book about a new immigrant's loneliness and the positive effect of retaining customs brought from the country of origin.
— Black Line Master #20

PROCEDURES

□ Discuss the experience of newly arrived immigrants, giving students enough time to share their feelings and thoughts. The following questions can be used as a starting point.
   — Have you ever moved from one city to another or from one country to another? If so, what were some of the things that you had to leave behind?

- Did you find moving a difficult experience? If so, why?
- Did you have any expectations and/or fears when you were moving? If so, what were they?
- Do you think your expectations and/or fears are shared by others who move? By all new arrivals to Canada?
- What new things did you have to learn when you moved?
- How are the things that have to be learnt when moving from one city to another the same as the things that have to be learnt when moving from one country to another? How are they different?
- Did you take any of your own special family traditions with you when you moved?
- What are some examples of traditions and values which can be easily kept by people moving from another country to Canada? Are there some which people might find difficult to maintain in Canada? If so, give examples and reasons for the difficulty.

☐ Read *Michi's New Year* or a similar story and have the class answer the questions on Black Line Master #20 in their notebooks. Students should then share their answers orally with the class.

EXTENDED ACTIVITY #19

PROCEDURES

☐ Have students work in groups to research the New Year celebrations of different ethno-cultural groups. They should find out when in the year New Year is celebrated, what types of activities take place, and why New Year is important for each group.

☐ In addition to group discussion and library research, students can learn from presentations given by parents and/or community members invited to the class.

☐ Each group should prepare charts, including written information, and illustrations, describing their New Year. These can be displayed on the walls of the class and used for future reference during the year.

☐ You may choose to celebrate one or more of the New Years, as appropriate.

Calendars

MULTICULTURAL OBJECTIVES

Students should be able to:
— learn about different calendars;
— appreciate the importance of different calendars to the lives of people from various cultural groups.

SKILL OBJECTIVES

Students should be able to:
— design and illustrate calendars;
— write tales;
— compare calendars.

RESOURCES

— Black Line Masters #21, #22, #23 and #24
— "A Fox, A Hen and A Bag of Rice" and "The Fox that Borrowed the Tiger's Authority" in *Fables and Legends from Ancient China*, by Shiu L. Kong and Elizabeth Wong, or equivalent Chinese fable
— Parents, community members

PROCEDURES

A) Gregorian Calendar

☐ Introduce the Gregorian calendar, which is in common use in Canada. You may explore topics such as the derivation of the names of the months and of the days of the week, the rationale for the division of the year and so on. (See Black Line Master #21 for a brief description of various calendars)

B) Chinese Calendar

☐ Provide students with a copy of Black Line Master #21, "Calendars and Zodiacs" and Black Line Master #22, "The Chinese Zodiac". Go over the calender as a group.

☐ If possible, invite a member of the local Chinese Canadian community to the class to give a short talk on the Chinese calendar.

☐ Use information on Black Line Master #23 to elaborate on the Chinese calendar. Then have students consider the following questions:
   — Are there any common characteristics between the animals chosen for the Chinese calendar?
   — Do the characteristics given for each animal fit what you know of the animal? Why or why not?
   — Under which animal sign were your born?
   — Do the characteristics of "your" animal fit your personality?
   — What can we learn about a people from its calendar?

☐ Divide the class into small groups and have each group design its own zodiac calendar, using other animals. They should describe the characteristics of each of the twelve animals chosen. Each group should then present its calendar to the class, along with the animal characteristics. Encourage the class to ask questions about why the group chose particular animals and how they determined the characteristics. Display the calendars on the bulletin board.

C) Chinese Fables and The Chinese Calendar

☐ Write the following questions on the board for students to consider while you read aloud the fables ''A Fox, a Hen and a Bag of Rice'' and ''The Fox that Borrowed the Tiger's Authority''.
  — What animal from the Chinese calendar is portrayed in the fable?
  — Are there animals in the fable which are not part of the Chinese calendar? Which one(s)?
  — Do the animals in the fable have the same characteristics or qualities as those that are listed for them in the Chinese calendar? Give examples.

☐ Maintain the same groups as above, and appoint a recorder to write down the group's answers to the questions. Groups should then present their answers to the class.

☐ Ask each group to write and illustrate its own tale, featuring animals from the Chinese zodiac calendar or others of their own choice, as the main characters. Display these, along with zodiacs and calendars, on the bulletin board.

EXTENDED ACTIVITY #20
_____

PROCEDURES

☐ Expand upon student's knowledge of calendars, using Black Line Master #24, ''Calendars'' along with appropriate books and encyclopedias. Students should consider questions such as the following:
  — What are some of the similarities and differences between the Chinese and Gregorian calendars?
  — What are some other types of calendars?
  — Which calendar is used internationally?
  — Do you and your family follow another calendar, as well as the Gregorian? If so, why and in what ways?
  — What year is it for (a) Chinese (b) Jewish (c) Hindu and (d) other communities

☐ Invite parents and representatives from various ethno-cultural communities to visit the class and talk about their calendar. Students should then make their own illustrated version of each calendar and display them on the bulletin board.

Is This Fair? Does Justice Prevail?

Cultures may interpret justice in different ways. You may find yourself dealing with issues and outcomes which are deemed by others as unjust within our Canadian tradition. At the same time, you may discover that some of our concerns and actions appear unjust within the context of other cultures. The key is to find responses within the Canadian democratic tradition and its laws and practice.

MULTICULTURAL OBJECTIVES

Students should be able to:
— appreciate that all people must deal with the struggle between justice and injustice and are concerned that justice prevails.

SKILL OBJECTIVES

Students should be able to:
— define terms;
— understand the components of a fable;
— compare two fables (Extended Activity #21);
— write and perform a play (Extended Activity #21).

RESOURCES

— "The Tiger, The Brahmin and The Jackal", in *Indian Fairy Tales* by Joseph Jacobs
— "Make your own Judgments" in *Fables and Legends from Ancient China* by Shiu L. Kong and Elizabeth Wong, or other fable which underscores fairness in our daily lives.

PROCEDURES

☐ Ask students to define the terms fairness and justice.

☐ Examine the characteristics of the fable. Direct the discussion to elicit the following:
　　— a fable has a moral;
　　— in a fable, animals are given human qualities;
　　— at the end of a fable, fairness and justice prevail

☐ Read "The Tiger, The Brahmin, and the Jackal" or its equivalent. Use questions like the following to discuss the fable.
　　— What human characteristics do the animals possess?
　　— What kind of people do the various animals represent?
　　— What lesson can we learn from the fable?
　　— What human characteristics do the animals represent?
　　— How does fairness and justice prevail in the fable?

EXTENDED ACTIVITY #21

PROCEDURE

☐ Ask children to write and perform a play based on "The Tiger, the Brahmin and the Jackal" or its equivalent.

☐ Divide the class into groups of 3-4 and give each group two fables to read aloud, taking turns amongst themselves. These could be "The Tiger, the Brahmin and the Jackal" and "Make Your Own Judgments" or their equivalents. Students should then compare

*Formal debates provide an
excellent way of encouraging
students to examine all sides of
an issue. They can be used to
special advantage when dealing
with situations in which
cultural differences lead to
different interpretations of
events and ideas.*

the two stories, using criteria such as: the main characters; the
Sage or Wise Man; the plot; the reason for the Sage's interven-
tion; the moral; whether fairness and justice prevailed. Have
them write their comparison in chart form and share their information with the class. Make a chart on the board incorporating
the points made by each group.

☐ Explore with the class whether justice ALWAYS prevails in the
end. Have them think of situations when it appears to, and
others when it does not. Encourage students to think of situations
from their own lives, from history, in the news. Examples might
include the internment of Japanese Canadians during World War
II, terrorism, slavery, aboriginal land claims.

ACTIVITY #22

Telling Our Own Tales

*Rememember that just about
everyone has a tale from their
childhood that they can recall.
You may well find that several
versions of the same tale are
told, providing scope for
interesting comparisons.*

*As an extension of the
activities on folk tales, fables
and fairy tales, a teacher asked
students in her grade 5/6 class
to find family members or
elders from their community to
tell them a tale which came
from their culture. They wrote
down these tales and read
them to the class. The class
discussed the stories in detail,
noting cultural traits which
were specific to each group, as
well as those which were
universal. A class book containing the tales was put
together as a wind up to the
work done.*

MULTICULTURAL OBJECTIVES

Students should be able to:

— identify and share common values across cultures;
— learn more about other cultures through their folk stories.

SKILL OBJECTIVES

Students should be able to:

— write stories;
— edit stories;
— work cooperatively in pairs.

RESOURCES

— work developed in Activities #20 and #21

PROCEDURES

☐ Review the fable, folk and fairy tale as literary forms. Then ask
each student to choose one and write their own. They can use a
Canadian setting, or set the story in their country of origin.
Students should read their stories aloud. Have questions like the
following on the board for the class to discuss after each story has
been read.

— Is the story a fable, folk tale or fairy tale? Why?
— What is the theme?
— What lesson did you learn from the story?
— Is the message of the story universal?

☐ After all stories have been read, collect them and assign a partner
to each student. Working in pairs, students should edit and
perfect one another's work. Important parts of each story may be
illustrated. Collect the final versions for a combined class book.

Justice and Injustice in the News

Refer to the note on debating, Extended Activity #21

MULTICULTURAL OBJECTIVES

Students should be able to:
— develop a broad sense of justice and injustice, encompassing various cultures and countries.

SKILL OBJECTIVES

Students should be able to:
— find relevant articles in newspapers and magazines;
— work effectively in groups;
— think critically.

RESOURCES

— newspapers and magazines

PROCEDURES

☐ Review the meaning of justice versus injustice which was developed in Activity #21.

☐ Have students use newspapers and magazines over a period of several days to find articles which exemplify the theme of justice versus injustice.

☐ Divide the class into small groups. Have each group discuss the articles which they found and select one which best reflects the theme of justice versus injustice. Each group should then present the article, explaining the issues involved. Set aside time at the end of each presentation for questions from the class.

☐ Use a section of the class bulletin board for current events stories which deal with the question "Does Justice Prevail?". Assign students to change the articles on a regular basis.

Values and Religious Education and Multiculturalism

This section explores two areas of study, religious education and values/moral education.

Using the theme of Our Religious and Spiritual Traditions, students examine some of the religious beliefs and practices which shape identity and cultural development. The activities enable students to experience some of the religious traditions which form part of our multicultural society. As a result, students should:

— become aware of the variety of regular community observances in various religious traditions;
— develop respect for the diversity of religious and spiritual expression and observance in Canada.

In order to achieve these objectives, activities may involve students in direct contact with different religious traditions in their community. Teachers should become familiar with all of the religious affiliations of children in their class, keeping in mind that some families will have no affiliation.

Activities grouped under the theme Prejudice and Discrimination support the aim of Values Education curricula — the development of the student's moral reasoning. This theme has major significance in our multicultural and multiracial society. The activities are designed to help students:

— develop a caring, responsible attitude towards themselves and others;
— work their way through the various stages of moral development.

In order to facilitate the study of the complementary areas of religious and values/moral education, and to respect the religious and moral convictions of families, ask parents/guardians to complete the short questionnaire appearing on Black Line Master #25 before students get involved in the experiential component of this unit.

☐ Our Religious and Spiritual Traditions
  Activity #24 — Canada's Religious Mosaic
  Activity #25 — Our Religious Practices
  Activity #26 — My Religious Traditions
  Activity #27 — Visiting Houses of Worship

☐ Prejudice and Discrimination
    Activity #28 — Similar and Different
    Activity #29 — Are We Really Different?
    Activity #30 — Case Studies
    Activity #31 — Defending Our Rights

ACTIVITY #24

Canada's Religious Mosaic

This unit calls for extra-ordinary sensitivity and tact. You must be prepared to value a wide range of religious practices and traditions, accept that what is ''superstition'' to one may be an axiom of faith to another, and assist students in seeing all religious beliefs and systems as having equal dignity and merit. At the same time, you will need to acknowledge the reality and acceptability of NOT having a religious affiliation.

MULTICULTURAL OBJECTIVES

Students should be able to:
— understand different kinds of religious and other celebrations and practices in the community.

SKILL OBJECTIVES

Students should be able to:
— formulate and answer questions.

RESOURCES

— Mayled, Jon. *Religious Festivals*
— Parry, Caroline. *Let's Celebrate*
— Black Line Master #26

PROCEDURES

☐ Initiate a class discussion about some of the unique and special things various ethno-cultural groups contribute to Canadian life. Examples will include language, music, food, crafts and so on. If the class has completed the social studies and language arts sections, they will have research to draw upon. Direct the discussion to the different religious traditions and beliefs which people from various cultural groups have brought with them to Canada.

☐ Develop a general discussion dealing with religion. Pose questions like the following:
    — What is religion?
    — What is the relationship between religion and various celebrations?
    — What are examples of celebrations which are not religious?

☐ Ask the class to name some world religions and list their replies on the board. Complete the list as necessary, noting for each one its place of worship, spiritual leader, name(s) for its god(s), major celebrations. You may hand out copies of Black Line Master #26 and have students complete the chart from class or small group discussion or research.

☐ Discuss the system of belief common to aboriginal people in Canada, pointing out that some practice Christianity while keeping their faith in the traditional ways. Indicate the links between the traditional spirituality of Native Canadians and that of other aboriginal peoples, showing that theirs too is a world religion.

Our Religious Practices

Keeping in mind that the family has the major responsibility for teaching religion, make a special effort to bring into the classroom parents or elders of the community to explain specific festivals and/or demonstrate and share religious ceremonies.

This activity can be expanded in many different ways. One teacher developed a unit based on Extended Activity #19, focusing on how different ethno-cultural groups celebrated New Year. Similar units could be developed around the seasons, harvest time, festivals of lights and so on.

MULTICULTURAL OBJECTIVES

Students should be able to:
— understand the religious traditions of various groups.

SKILL OBJECTIVES

Students should be able to:
— formulate and answer questions;
— recall details.

RESOURCES

— Black Line Master #25 (if you have not previously sent it home) and #27
— parents and/or community resource people
— filmstrip projector, cassette player, VCR or movie projector (as required by presenters)
— multicultural and multi-religious calendars
— Mayled, Jon. *Religious Festivals*
— Paper, Jordan. *Offering Smoke: The Sacred Pipe and Native American Religion*
— Parry, Caroline. *Let's Celebrate*
— *Pictorial Charts Education Trust*
— *Pictorial Wallcharts*
— *Religions of the World Series*

PROCEDURES

☐ Send home copies of Black Line Master #25 (if you have not already done so). Contact the parents who indicated their willingness to visit the class to demonstrate and share their religious celebrations and observances. Try to put together a list of volunteers who can present unique aspects of a variety of religions. If there are significant gaps in your list, contact a religious institution, ethno-cultural community centre or inter-faith centre for help. Ensure that a representative of aboriginal spirituality is included. Try contacting a native friendship centre or community resource for suggestions.

☐ Meet or speak with presenters to go over the content they will be covering, as well as such details as dates, grade level and time allotment. Encourage them to bring along slides, films and/or artifacts.

☐ Invite all of the parents to share the experience with their children. (see sample invitation, Black Line Master #27)

☐ Prepare the class before each presentation by using some of the resources listed. Encourage the class to jot down questions during the presentations which they can ask during the question and answer period.

☐ Display the room with materials brought in by the visitors or put up the charts listed in the resource list.

My Religious Tradition

Here, as elsewhere, be alert to the potential for variety within the various traditions, and the possibility of differences within families with regard to religious affiliation and practices. Encourage children with no religious affiliation to participate by learning about other traditions and/or sharing a celebration that may be especially meaningful to them.

After completing a study of various religions, a teacher asked students to compare their religion with another whose practices were quite different from their own. This project included student-teacher contracts, crosswords, "wonderwords", and word lists pertaining to religions.

MULTICULTURAL OBJECTIVES

Students should be able to:
— share information about their religious traditions with the class.

SKILL OBJECTIVES

Students should be able to:
— organize ideas into an oral presentation;
— speak effectively to the class.

RESOURCES
— *Pictorial Charts Educational Trust*
— *Pictorial Wallcharts*
— Materials brought by students, eg. posters, traditional dress, artifacts

PROCEDURES

☐ In Activity #25, resource people presented aspects of their religious traditions. In this activity, students are the presenters, while family members and others are the invited guests.

☐ Have students select a festival or religious practice which was not presented in Activity #25. Encourage them to use various media, wear traditional dress, bring in religious objects and use other techniques to make their presentations as effective as possible. They may also use the charts listed above to illustrate their talk.

☐ Set dates, then allot time for preparations and for making invitations to relatives and community members. Review the presentations with each child, checking content, "props" and length (not more than 30 minutes).

☐ Follow each presentation with a question and answer time.

Visiting Houses of Worship

MULTICULTURAL OBJECTIVES

Students should be able to:
— develop an understanding of and appreciation for the places of worship and community life of people of various religious affiliations and cultural origins.

SKILL OBJECTIVES

Students should be able to:
— demonstrate appropriate behaviour in places of worship;
— note details;
— fill in a questionnaire.

RESOURCES

— various houses of worship and native friendship centres
— Black Line Master #27

PROCEDURES

☐ Once students understand and appreciate some of the religions which are part of the religious mosaic of their class, city, province and country, contact a resource person from a variety of places of worship (Christian church, Jewish synagogue or temple, Hindu or Buddhist temple, Islamic mosque) to arrange for class visits.

☐ Before each visit, hand out the questionnaire (Black Line Master #27) and go over the questions, adding any that students suggest. Prepare students to behave with appropriate decorum and respect during the visit.

☐ After each visit, have students share the answers to their questionnaires and compare student responses. Put together a class collage for each visit, using the sketches and written impressions.

ACTIVITY #28

Similar and Different

People can feel and demonstrate prejudice against a multitude of things, including a particular religion, gender, nation, language, colour, or ethnic group.

MULTICULTURAL OBJECTIVES

Students should be able to:
— accept similarities and differences as an integral part of human experience;
— avoid making judgement based on appearances.

SKILL OBJECTIVES

— make reasoned judgements.

RESOURCES

— 2 familiar fruits such as an orange, apple, grapes
— 2 grapefruits, one white, one red
— 1 unfamiliar fruit, such as persimmon, lychee, tamarind, papaya

PROCEDURE

☐ Ensure that students understand the meaning of the words similar and different. Ask them to define the terms and provide examples.

☐ Show the class two familiar fruits (excluding grapefruits) and ask them to compare them, using criteria such as colour, size, shape, smell. List their answers on a chart.

☐ Next, show them an unfamiliar fruit. Pass it around so students can touch and smell it. Then ask questions like the following:
   — Can you describe the inside of the fruit without opening it up?
   — Can you compare this fruit with one of the familiar fruits you looked at before?
   — Would you be willing to taste this unfamiliar fruit? If not, why not?

☐ You may want to present other unfamiliar fruits and ask the same questions. When you observe that the point has been made, as the following questions:
   — Are we able to judge things from their external appearance?
   — Are these kinds of judgments valid ones?
   — Would you want to be judged by your appearance alone?

☐ Bring out the 2 grapefruits. Ask students if they look the same from the outside. Have them describe what they think each looks like on the inside. Then open both so students see that they are different colours. Students should be led to the generalization that although objects look the same on the outside, they may be very different on the inside. Have students make up their own cautions against making judgments without first looking beyond the exterior.

EXTENDED ACTIVITY #28

RESOURCES
— *The New Kid.* (Video)
— Pasternak, Carol and Allen Sutterfield. *Stone Soup.*
— Wallace, Ian and Angela Wood. *The Sandwich.*
— Any other material which deals with "different" food habits.

PROCEDURE
☐ Use one or more of the resources as a starting point for a discussion about prejudice and discrimination surrounding food.
☐ Try to organize a meal at which a variety of "different" foods are served.

Are We Really Different?

MULTICULTURAL OBJECTIVES

Students should be able to:
— recognize that similarities and differences are an integral part of the human experience;
— be sensitive to the harm caused by discrimination;
— develop harmonious relationships.

SKILL OBJECTIVES

Students should be able to:
— analyze the meaning of a song or poem;
— view films and/or filmstrips critically;
— develop solutions for problems.

RESOURCES

— *Black Fugitive.* (Filmstrip)
— *Childhood Memories of a Japanese Canadian — Lost Years.* (Filmstrip)
— *Gurdeep Singh Bains.* (Film)
— *Josiah Henson — A Remarkable Black Canadian.* (Film)
— Lennon, John. *Imagine.* (Song)
— Stevens, Ray. *Everything is Beautiful.* (Song)
— *Teacher, They Called Me a _____. Prejudice and Discrimination in the Classroom*

PROCEDURES

☐ Play a recording of a song like "Everything is Beautiful" or "Imagine" or read a poem stressing love, harmony and acceptance. Discuss it with the class, using questions like the following:
   — Do you like the words?
   — What is the theme or message?
   — Do you think that we can live the message?
   — In what ways do we stray from the message? (for example, showing prejudice against people because of their gender, religion, colour or origin)

☐ Ask the class to suggest what we can do to make our world as beautiful as the one described in the song or poem. List their answers on the board.

☐ Show the films and film strips in the resource list, without lead-in or explanation. Simply ask the students to put themselves in the place of the main characters.

☐ At the end of the films, ask students the following questions
   — What problems did the main characters face in each film?
   — What part did other people play in causing these problems?
   — How were these problems worked out?
   — What would YOU have done if faced by the same problems?

— In which ways did people discriminate against others? (religion, ethnic origin, colour, physical appearance, clothes, food preferences)
— How does discrimination really hurt people?
— In what ways are people fundamentally the same?

Case Studies

MULTICULTURAL OBJECTIVES

Students should be able to:
— understand the meaning and negative impact of prejudice and discrimination;
— work towards resolving conflicts and inequalities arising from prejudice and discrimination.

SKILL OBJECTIVES

Students should be able to:
— analyze a case study;
— infer meaning from a case study;
— develop solutions for a problem.

RESOURCES

— Black Line Master #28

PROCEDURES

☐ Divide the class into groups and give each student a copy of the case study on Black Line Master #28. Have them read the case and discuss it in their groups.

☐ Ask each group to identify the issue and to suggest ways to help resolve it. Each group should then share their solution with the class and work towards a consensus.

☐ Groups could then write their own case study illustrating incidents of prejudice and discrimination for class discussion.

Defending Our Rights

MULTICULTURAL OBJECTIVES

Students should be able to:
— understand and respect the basic rights of Canadians.

Students should be able to:
— think critically;
— understand their own potential as agents of change.

RESOURCES
— Canadian Charter of Rights and Freedoms
— Canadian Human Rights Act (and related provincial legislation)
— *Childhood Memories of a Japanese Canadian — Lost Years.* Filmstrip.
— *The House at 12 Rose Street.* (Film)
— *Overture — Linh from Viet Nam.* (Film)
— *Teach Me to Dance.* (Film)
— Black Line Master #30

PROCEDURES
☐ Begin by examining the meaning of the concept of human rights (see Glossary)

☐ Article #15 of the Canadian Charter of Rights and Freedoms states "Every individual is equal before and under the law and has the right to the equal protection and equal benefit of the law without discrimination and, in particular, without discrimination based on race, national or ethnic origin, colour, religion, sex, age or mental or physical disability."

Read it aloud and discuss its meaning, using examples. Ask students to think of any instances where their rights or the rights of others have been violated.

☐ Show the films and filmstrip to illustrate violations of our basic rights and freedoms. They show how various forms of prejudice and discrimination negatively affect our relationships and undermine our basic rights. Ask students to identify which basic rights have been violated in each film. Then have them suggest how positive attitudes and actions could have changed the situations in each story.

☐ Help students recognize that prejudice and discrimination, and subsequent violations of rights, are often handed down from one generation to another. Today's young people can change this situation by realizing that their values and actions will be the heritage of future generations.

APPENDIX

Black Line Masters

#		Page
1	Letter to Parents/Guardians	56
2	Who Am I	57
3	My Family Tree	60
4	Ethnic Origins	61
5	Most Frequently Reported Ethnic Origins	62
6	Non-British, Non-French Ethnic Origins	63
7	Immigration by Source	64
8	Aboriginal Origins	65
9	Visible Minority Groups	66
10	Making a New Life	67
11	I'd Like to be an Immigrant	72
12	My Home, My Home	73
13	New Immigrants and New Explorers	74
14	Names can be Similar but Different	75
15	Learning about Our Names	77
16	Naming Customs	79
17	Questions about Naming Customs	80
18	How We Can Help	82
19	Teach me to Fly, Skyfighter	84
20	Michi's New Year	85
21	Calendars and Zodiacs	86
22	The Chinese Zodiac	87
23	In which Year were you Born?	88
24	Calendars	89
25	Parent/Guardian Questionnaire	91
26	Major Religions of the World	92
27	Visiting Places of Worship	93
28	Case Study: Prejudice and Discrimination	95

Annotated Resource List

	Page
Books	
Fiction	96
Non-Fiction	98
Charts, Games, and Kits	99
Films and Videos	100
Filmstrips and Audio Cassettes	101
Reference Books and Other Publications	102

Dear Parent/Guardian,

This coming school year your child will be involved in a learning process where multicultural activities have been integrated into the regular school curriculum. These multicultural activities have been designed to meet the learning objectives as outlined for the following subject areas: Social Studies, Language Arts and Values and Religious Education.

It is expected that this approach to your child's education will both meet the general requirements of the programs of study and prepare your child to live more effectively in our multicultural/multiracial Canadian society.

Your cooperation and support in making this educational experience a success will be appreciated.

Thank you very much.

Sincerely,

Who am I?

My Personal World:

My name is _____

I was born in _____
(place of birth-town, city, country)

I live in _____
(town, city)

There are _____ people in my family: _____ brothers, _____ sisters,

_____ others.

My Cultural World:

LANGUAGE

I can speak or understand the following language(s):

speak _____ understand _____

In my family, some of my relatives can speak or understand the following language(s):

_____

If I had a chance I would like to learn to speak _____
(name of language)

because _____

_____

In my opinion, knowing how to speak more than one language is important because

_____

_____

_____

FOOD

Each week, the foods I eat most often are:

_____ _____ _____

On certain occasions my family eats foods such as _____ that are special to my cultural group.

My favourite special foods are _____

CLOTHING

In summer I usually wear _____

In winter I usually wear _____

Member of my family wear _____
which is/are special to our cultural group.

They wear these clothes only on _____
(describe or name occasions)

or always _____
(yes)   (no)

MUSIC

My favourite kind of music is _____

Other members of my family enjoy _____
(describe or name kinds of music)

I can play the _____

Other members of my family can play the _____

If I had a chance, I would like to learn to play the _____

because _____

DANCE

I have seen kinds of dancing called _____

I have seen this kind of dancing at _____
(name of place and occasion).

I am able to dance the _____

My favourite kind of dance is _____

If I had a chance, I would like to learn to dance the _____ because

_____

CELEBRATIONS/HOLIDAYS

My favourite celebrations or special holidays are:

_____

My family celebrates _____, which is
special to our cultural group. During these special celebrations/holidays, it is customary to

_____
(describe what is done, eaten, worn, etc.).

_____

_____

_____

MY CULTURE

This is how I would describe my cultural heritage:

_____

_____

_____

_____

My Family's World:

My father's name is _____

He was born in _____

He lives in _____

My mother's name is _____

She was born in _____

She lives in _____

Our favourite family activity is _____

My Family Tree

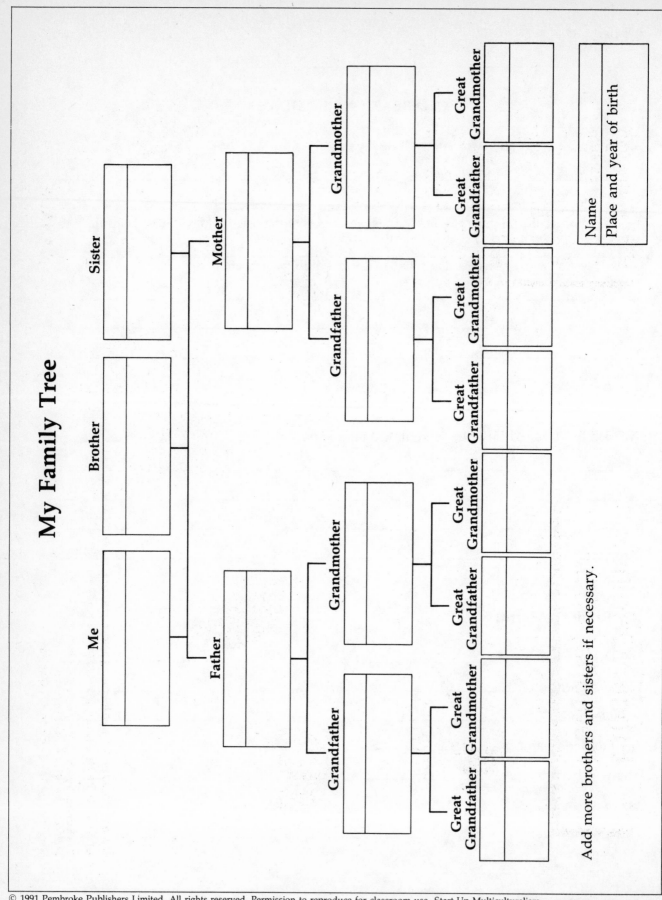

Me

Brother

Sister

Father

Mother

Grandfather

Grandmother

Grandfather

Grandmother

Great Grandfather

Great Grandmother

Great Grandfather

Great Grandmother

Great Grandfather

Great Grandmother

Great Grandfather

Great Grandmother

Name

Place and year of birth

Add more brothers and sisters if necessary.

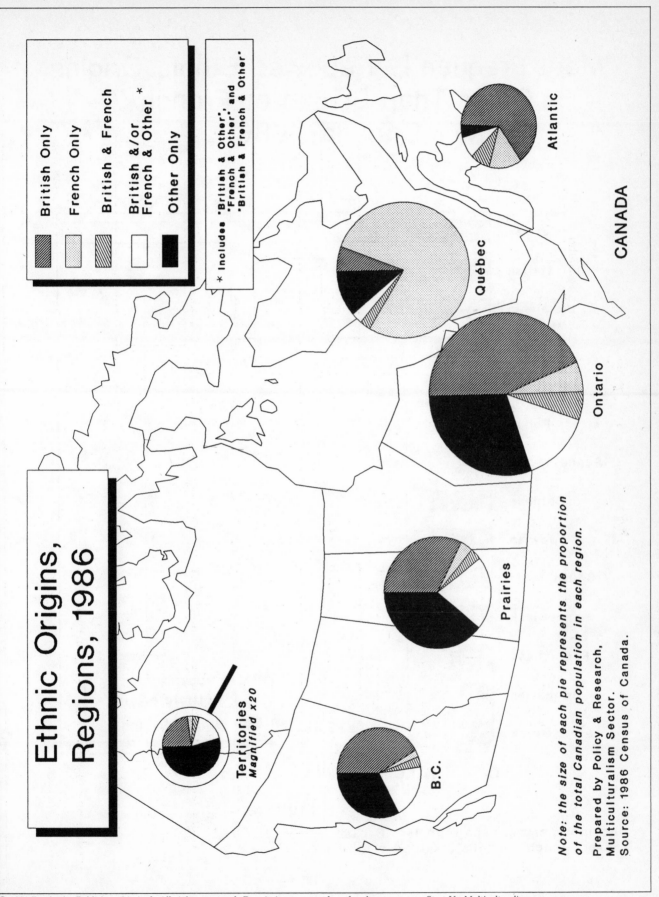

Ethnic Origins, Regions, 1986

Legend:
- ▨ British Only
- ▦ French Only
- ▧ British & French
- ☐ British &/or French & Other *
- ■ Other Only

* Includes "British & Other", "French & Other", and "British & French & Other".

Atlantic

Québec

Ontario

Prairies

B.C.

Territories
Magnified x20

CANADA

Note: the size of each pie represents the proportion of the total Canadian population in each region.

Prepared by Policy & Research,
Multiculturalism Sector.
Source: 1986 Census of Canada.

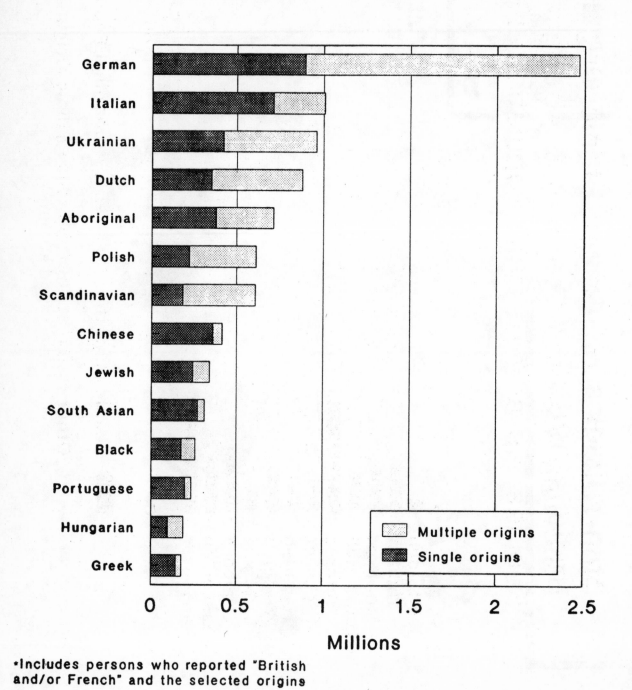

Most Frequently Reported Ethnic Origins Other Than British or French*, Canada, 1986

German
Italian
Ukrainian
Dutch
Aboriginal
Polish
Scandinavian
Chinese
Jewish
South Asian
Black
Portuguese
Hungarian
Greek

0   0.5   1   1.5   2   2.5

Millions

Multiple origins
Single origins

*Includes persons who reported "British and/or French" and the selected origins

Non-British, Non-French Ethnic Origins, Showing Visible Minorities & Aboriginal Peoples, as a % of CMA Population, 1986

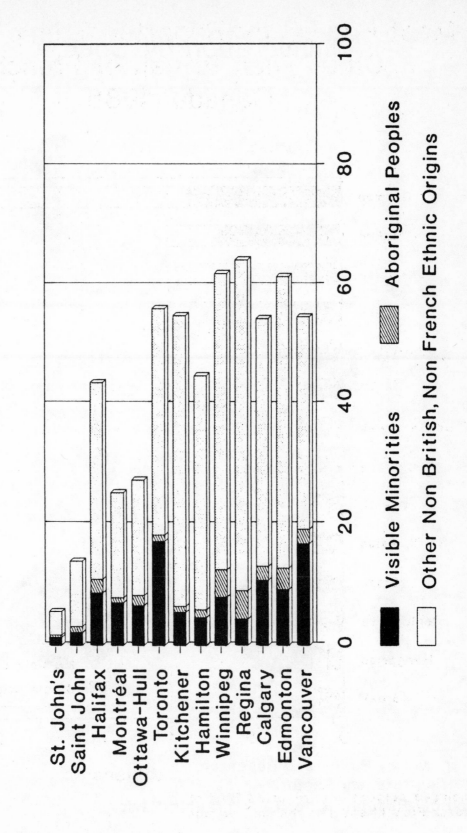

Visible Minorities

Aboriginal Peoples

Other Non British, Non French Ethnic Origins

Immigration by Source

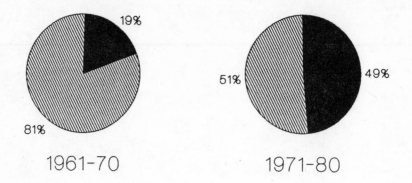

1961-70   1971-80

Africa, Asia, Caribbean
Latin, Central and South America

Europe, United States, Australia
New Zealand

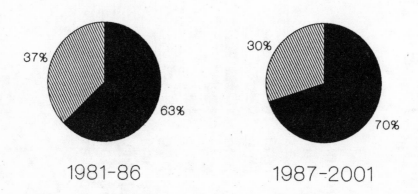

1981-86   1987-2001

**Prepared by Policy and Research,
Multiculturalism Sector
Source: Beaujot, R. for Demographic Review**

% Regional Population Reporting
Aboriginal Origins
Canada and Regions, 1986

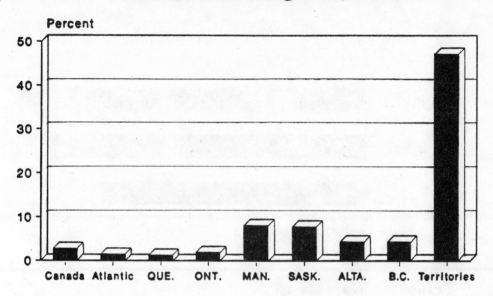

Distribution of Aboriginal Population,
Provinces & Territories, 1986

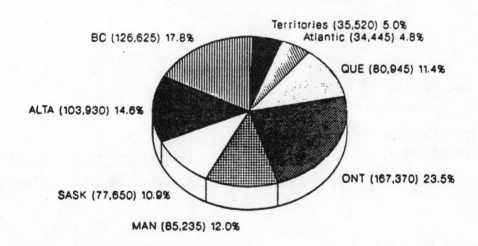

**Prepared by Policy & Research,
Multiculturalism Sector.
Source: 1986 Census of Canada.**

Visible Minority Groups, Canada, 1986

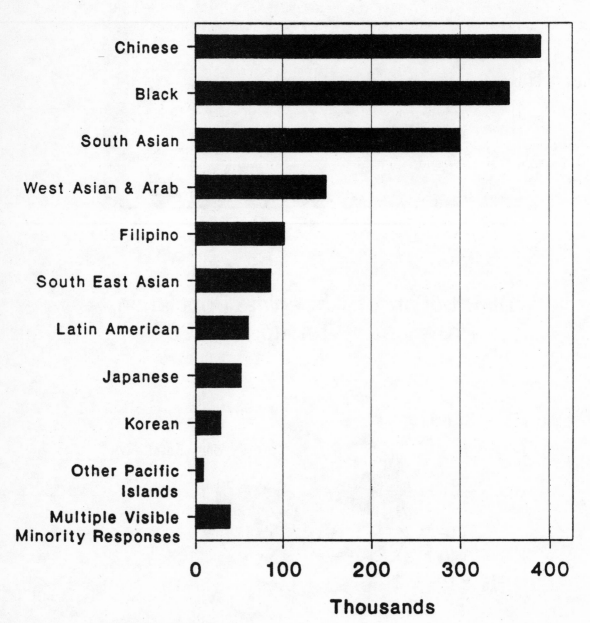

Prepared by Policy & Research,
Multiculturalism Sector.
Source: 1986 Census of Canada.

Making a New Life

The following stories describe what it feels like to come to Canada as an immigrant. As you read each story, think of how the experiences of the person telling the story are similar to or different from those of other immigrants.

Pulling Up Roots

When my father came to Canada, my mother didn't want to come. So my father came and told my aunt to come, and my aunt told my grandfather to come, and my grandfather told my grandmother to come. And now my mother wanted to come, but she couldn't because my other grandmother was almost dying. My mother has to look after her.

My father felt sad and so did I because I can't see her. And in the summer I went and saw my mom. And the saddest part was when I had to come back to Canada. I wish I could go to Portugal again. My mother has to look after my grandmother.

* * *

My grandfather lives in Hong Kong. He is ninety-eight years old. He is good. Sometimes he took me to the playground to play. I like my grandfather but my father said, ''We will go to Canada,'' so I came to Canada. I can't ever play with him.

* * *

It was a very difficult decision for me to leave my country. My cultural background was such that we were very attached to the family. We were a very, very tight unit. Maybe it's difficult for a person in the West to understand this, but even a grown-up child, a son, always lives at home. If he marries he brings another member into the family. The daughters go out. When they are married they go with their husbands. But the sons stay at home. That made it difficult for me.

Why We Came and Where We Came From

We came to Canada because where we used to live in Greece was poor. We had a poor house. Then my father came to Canada because he thought we wouldn't be poor. He came here by himself when it was October 4, 1975, and he found a job and a house. He was writing letters to us. Then he told us to come to Canada. We left about 5:00 in the morning. We went with a taxi to a city and we took a Greek plane and we landed in Athens, a very big city. We took a small bus and it took us to the plane. The plane was called CP Air.

* * *

September the 11th, 1973. In Chile soldiers killed the President. They burned down the house where the President lived. The windows were broken. It had a flag on top and the flag was burning like it was just paper.

Every day my mother had to go to the embassy and she said, ''Please, I want to see my husband. Please, could you sign this for me please?''

Every day the man said, ''*No.*''

We saw the soldiers putting cannons and machine guns and rifles and guns and all those things in the ground of the beach.

After all those things we went to Honduras and now we are here. We like

Canada. We have friends, we learn English and we are happy here. But I like it better there. I'm sad because we cannot be in Chile. I miss my friends, my grandmother, and I hope we would go back in a little while when the soldiers are gone.

* * *

I came from Lebanon. Lebanon is a small country. They speak four languages: Arabic, French, English, and Armenian. I speak some Arabic, some French. Armenian is my language and I am learning English now. There is a war in Lebanon now, and that is why I came to Canada. In Lebanon most of the time they speak Arabic because Lebanon is an Arabic country.

* * *

We came to Canada because Hong Kong is a small island and there are too many people living there. They don't have many parks and fields or grass. A lot of dirty things come out of the trucks that go by. The traffic is always stuck and the lake is dirty and the streets are dirty, too.

Where we lived, the drivers of the cars and trucks kept on pushing their horns and made a lot of noise every Sunday. Every Sunday they had horse racing, and because our building was right beside the horse track, there was a lot of noise.

A Whole New World

Sven: It was a whole new world. What I remember most of Victoria in those first weeks was the different smell in the stores. I suppose it was the different kinds of vegetables. I remember that very well. The whole world smelt different.

Annie: The food was *so* different. Even the meat had a different taste. You had to get used to all new things.

* * *

It was not easy to live in a new land at my age. But my daughter and her family are here and I like to be with them, especially if I can be of some use. I went to English classes but it was very difficult. My tongue and my head are not built for the strange new sounds. The first six months I was here, I didn't get on a bus or a streetcar alone, I was so afraid. My whole world had been turned upside down.

* * *

We went through some pretty rough times here. But you have to start somewhere. Not speaking the language made it much more difficult. I could have bought some stuff on credit — groceries, something for the kitchen. And then I could have paid it off when I got the money. But I didn't have the language to ask.

We starved quite a bit. With no reason. There's no reason to starve in this country. But we didn't speak the language and there was no way you could go in and ask for help. I remember the first store we went into here to buy groceries. We wanted eggs. Oh, my god, how to explain? Finally we had to do this "Cucu, cucu, cucu." (He bends his arms and flaps them like a chicken, all the time roaring with laughter.) I'm not kidding. We had to sit on a box and "cucu, cucu." It was the only way. The only way.

Getting a Job

It helps to come here with a vision. We knew what we wanted. We had a goal to work toward. For us, it wasn't that hard. I am coming out of a bakery. My father was a baker too. For about three years I worked in different bakeries here, but our idea was always to start a bakery of our own.

* * *

There is no work and yet you must put food on the table, put a roof over your head and clothes on your body. My wife has had no work for seven months. I had a job with the city last summer cutting grass in city parks. Now I'm on unemployment. I get $75 a week. It's not enough money to live. We want work. Any kind of work. I can get back that job with the city in April, but I must find something until then.

* * *

I feel fulfilled here. I have a job in a factory. It's not a very good job but I am able to help my family financially and that makes me feel good. My husband is a chemical engineer but he does not speak the language and he must work here as a welder.

* * *

I was already 45 when I came so that made it difficult. But I managed. I'm a graduate accountant but because of the lack of English I had to work as a labourer. I didn't speak a word of English when I came. I worked first in greenhouses as I have a heavy background in horticulture. For 17 years I was an accountant in the Department of Agriculture in Yugoslavia.

Of course I went to English class when I came. I worked very hard. I went to professional courses, too, other than straight language classes. I had to learn a technical English. I felt frustrated, of course, that I couldn't just go on with my profession when I came here. But that is the problem of all professional immigrants. You have to rewrite exams, redo diplomas. But I was prepared for this before I came. I was ready. I considered this as a sacrifice, as a price I had to pay to emigrate. Finally, after I passed all sorts of exams at all levels, including a special five-year course in advanced accountancy, I had the qualification I needed.

* * *

My father works in a factory where they make leather jackets. My father cuts out jackets, then passes them to somebody else to sew them.

When he comes home from work, he just goes to the bathroom to take a bath. Then he eats, and then he goes to sleep.

My dad says that the job makes him tired and that he wants to get another job because his legs hurt from a job where you have to be standing up all day long.

* * *

A few years ago, while my father was still working in construction, he was breaking cement with a machine. One day while he was doing his job, the machine slipped off his hand and made a hole that almost went through his whole hand. But he didn't tell the Compensation Board. Neither did he tell his friends at work because he didn't want to have a layoff.

After work he went to the doctor and got four stitches. He kept going to work for a month and by then he was cured. That's how my father kept his job.

Friends, Neighbours, and School Life

. . . . . They learned English in the day care centre where there were children of all social classes, of all colours. They do well in school and have a lot of friends. However, life for a child in a family of immigrants is quite a bit more difficult than for a Canadian child. The immigrant child must cope with the fact that at home his parents speak to him in one way and teach him certain things, while at school he learns something that is often quite different. The children resent this. They are young and they don't want to be different. They don't even like their friends to know that their parents are Spanish, because in fights or disagreements it is often used to insult them.

* * *

. . . . .My little girl did not start to speak English until she was five and she started school. We spoke Italian all the time at home. The first month at school was difficult for her. But after that she was my teacher. If she had had her way, she would have talked Italian all the time at school in the beginning. Now, if she had her way, she wouldn't speak Italian at all. They change.

The children have a better chance than I did when I was little. They are freer. If they need something, there is always somebody to help you here. Here they respect you for what you are. If you need money and you have a good job, you go to the bank. You get it. Back home it is difficult to do that. A farmer can't get those things. You are always in a lower class. So I've decided that if my children can have a better chance because we live here, I will sacrifice anything I can for them.

* * *

I remember when my son first started school here. He was 10. He really suffered. He didn't want his father to go to school to pick him up. The other children would tease him because his father had a turban and a brown skin. He said they teased him, too, about his skin and he would just give them a left and a right. But when they said it about his father he felt very bad. The colour of your skin really makes a big difference here. A very big difference.

* * *

Sure, I've got a nice house here, a big car. In my own country I only could afford a motorbike. But so what? There's got to be more to your life than that. No one here cares too much about other people. It is very much a land where you say, "This is my business, don't you interfere. That is your business over there." Everyone has his own house, his own car, his own family. The idea seems to be you don't ask or tell or share. It's a no-no. After a while, you stop relying on your friends. You stop even asking of your family. You don't want to put them out. You don't want to cause them any trouble.

* * *

In my neighbourhood the houses have beautiful colours. They are made of bricks and they have porches. The backyards are very big and most of them have grape or peach trees and green grass. Most of the houses also have big trees in front of them. The parks are around two blocks away from the neighbourhood. The stores are also near and there are a lot of them.

There are many different kinds of people that live in my neighbourhood. There are Black, English, Chinese, Pakistani, Italian, and many more. They are all very friendly and kind and also helpful. My next door neighbours are Italian and they are very helpful to us and we are helpful to them. We all get along very nice, most of us do.

I think my neighbourhood is beautiful and I love it, especially the people.

Parents and Children

I worry about the children. They have no one to kiss them and hug them and touch them. We are like that in Italy. We show our love like that. Here, nobody touches you. It is all different.

I really like it here. We got all the things we need . . . I suppose there is just one thing I could say about being a Canadian who wasn't exactly born here. It means you got all the benefits of being a Canadian but you always seem to be a bit on the outside. You're not quite the same as other people. Even if you try hard to be like them.

My mama and my papa are not like other parents of my friends. They speak pretty good English, not too much of an accent or anything. Especially my father. My mother gets a bit mixed up with the English grammar sometimes. But my father speaks perfect English. But it's not how he speaks, it's what he says and the way he looks. My father is a man who likes to talk. Everywhere he goes he starts to talk to people. Not stupid things that don't make sense. Just friendly. And he laughs a lot. Mama laughs too. She doesn't talk too much, but she laughs. And people don't always appreciate it. Most people on a bus here don't just start to talk to their neighbour. But my papa sits right down and starts to say something friendly . . . But you'd be amazed how many people just look at him like he's crazy. And they try to move away from him, so he won't bother them any more. But Papa doesn't really try to bother anyone. If they would know him they would know he just want to be friendly. That's the Mexican way, he tells me. ''A little bit of sunshine wherever you go. You can't go wrong that way.'' He's always saying that . . .

When I was little, I remember how much fun it always was with Papa. If I was somewhere there was a staircase, I could always slide down. He'd lift me up and hold me up all the way down. With him you always do things the fun way. But now — since I've been about 11 — I get a bit embarrassed sometimes. It's hard to always be so different from other people.

* * *

I am happy my kids are going to grow up in Canada. I wouldn't dream of taking them back and letting them live in Lebanon. In any shape or form that you want to look at it, I think Canada is the best country in the world. But there is one thing — the way they bring up their children here is a different way than we do ourselves. I'd like to bring up my children the same way they're bringing up their children, but there is something different in between . . .

I know my daughters will be mixing with the Canadian people. But still, in our home we keep training them and keep talking to them. We keep teaching them to be like Lebanese girls. Here in Canada if a girl is 16 years old and she doesn't have a boyfriend, the rest of the kids start laughing at her. There must be something wrong with you. But for us, a girl can have her friends, she can go out, but up to a certain point. After she's been out for so many hours she has to be back home. And she has to know exactly what she's doing.

It's different for a boy. A boy always has the authority to do what he wants. A boy takes responsibility no matter how young he is. Girls are different. You have to keep after them. You have to keep teaching them, giving them all your love and your idea of life all the time, before they get themselves into a mess. While the boys can understand you when they're 10 or 15 years old, the girls don't.

* * *

In the summer here lots of kids wear halters and culottes and sensible, cool clothes like that to school. But when I want to dress like that my parents have a fit. ''Girls in Latin America don't go to school like that,'' they say. ''Girls in our country show respect for their teachers,'' they tell me. I got so fed up with the girls in Latin America. I am Canadian now and I want to be like the others. Anyway, my parents are still thinking of Uruguay 10 years ago. I bet it's all changed now.

Adelphi, Jamaica

Dear Canadians,

My name is Annette. I am 11 years old. I live with my grandfather and grandmother at Adelphi, Jamaica. On our farm we have cows, goats, pigs, chickens, a donkey, and a dog. We grow sugar cane, mangoes, breadfruit, coconuts, and apples. My aunt moved to Canada a few years ago. She teaches grade five in a small town near Edmonton, Alberta. Last year, she sent me a picture of the Royal Mounted Police. They are all riding horses in a big circle and their red uniforms look very nice. At school we have a book about Canada. It has many pictures of Eskimos and igloos and polar bears. My cousin in Canada writes to me. She told me that in Canada some shops have over 20 different types flavors of ice cream. Also many hamburgers.

Maybe that is why there are so many fat people in Canada. Many Canadians visit Jamaica. They like our beaches. Canadians are big and tall and some are very fat. Once I saw a movie showing Canadians tapping maple syrup from trees. It is very cheap, but when they put it into bottles or make it into candy, then it is very expensive. My teacher says that Canada grows a lot of wheat which is made into delicious bread. There is no need to boil water before drinking it in Canada. There is lots of clean water. It comes from Niagara Falls.

I would like to know more about Canada. Someday, I'd like to come to live in Canada. I'd like to be an immigrant.

Your Jamaican friend,
Annette

My Home, My Home

Home was Hong Kong with grandpa,
grandma and many little cousins,
Hot crowded streets, with toy stands
and food stalls and steaming hot buns,
Hovering over them giant skyscrapers,
Beaches full of happy faces and sun-burnt
children, splashing in the water;
A ride in the tram and once even in a
rickshaw, and a car ferry across the
harbour.

Canada is new, different, spacious and
Oh, very cold.
Calgary is nice, with snow-capped
mountains and beautiful Banff.
Calgary is 'Hi' from a friendly neighbour,
The Stampede, under the hot sun,
sticky candy floss all over your face,
The excitement of the rodeo and
chuckwagon races.

Calgary is being bundled up in heavy
clothing, with frosted nose and face,
Skating with friends in winter frolics.
Calgary is having new pets, yelping and
romping in the large backyard.
Calgary is now home, and a happy one too.

I-Syin, 9 years old

New Immigrants and New Explorers

Topics to Include in Travel Log:

1. Reasons for leaving country of origin

_____

_____

_____

2. Preparation and date of departure

_____

_____

3. Travel plan

_____

_____

_____

4. High points and low points during the journey

_____

_____

_____

5. Date and place of arrival

_____

6. First impressions upon arrival

_____

_____

_____

7. High points and low points in days of early settlement

_____

_____

Names Can be Similar But Different

If the students in your class have different cultural backgrounds, there will probably be a wide variety of first and last names on your class list. Several people in your class may share the same first name. Maybe somebody else in your class, school, or community has the same family name as yours but is not related to you. Have you ever wondered how names began? Do you know why some names are more popular than others? Have you noticed that some names have a special meaning?

Some first names are more common than others. The name "John" is the most popular boy's name in many parts of the world. Like many other first names, John was taken from the Bible. In Hebrew, John is **Yohanan**, which means "God is gracious". The name John changes from country to country or from language to language.

John	(English)
Ian, Iain	(Scottish)
Sean, Shane	(Irish)
Evan	(Welsh)
Jean	(French)
Hans, Johannes	(German)
Johan	(Swedish, Norwegian)
Johann	(Swiss)
Hansel	(Austrian)
Jan	(Dutch)
Jens	(Danish)
Giovanni	(Italian)
Ivan	(Russian, Ukrainian)
Ioannes, Jannis	(Greek)
Juan	(Spanish)
Joaninho	(Brazilian)
Iban	(Basque)
Yuhanna	(Turkish)
Yohanna	(Arabic)
Yohan	(Thai)
Yohana-Den	(Japanese)
Yahya	(Moroccan)

Some family names are more popular than others. The most common name in European language is some form of "Smith," which means a person who works with iron. This is what "Smith" looks like in different languages:

Le Fèvre, La Farge, La Forge, Fernand	(French)
Ferrari, Fabbri, Fabroni, Ferraio	(Italian)
Herrera, Herrero, Hernández, Fernández	(Spanish)
Ferreiro, Ferreira	(Portuguese)
Schmidt, Schmied	(German)
Smed	(Swedish)
Kuznetsoz	(Russian)
Kováć	(Czech)
Kovács	(Hungarian)
Kovac	(Bulgarian)
Kowak, Kowalski	(Polish)
Haddad	(Lebanese and Syrian Arabic)
Magoon	(Irish)

Different cultures developed different rules for forming last names or family names. In many cultures, children take the father's last name. Some family names have an ending which means "son of". In some cultures, these endings have different forms for male and female children. For example:

Scandinavian	Johann**son**, Jen**sen**
Russian	Ivan**ov**, Ivan**ovna** (ovna = daughter of)
Spanish	Martin**ez**
Polish	Kowal**ski** Kowal**ska** (ska = daughter of) Bohadano**wicz**, Bohdanowicz**owa** (owa = daughter of)

German .... Turp**itz**
Greek .... Asimako**poulos** (poulos = "little bird of")
Chinese .... Mao **Tse**-tung (Family name "Mao" is written first)

In Scottish, Irish, and English, "of" comes before not after the father's name:

Scottish .... **Mac**Gregor, **Mc**Neill, **M'**Leod
Irish .... **O'**Shea, **O'**Reilly, **O'**Rourke
English .... **Fitz**roy (fitz = son, roy or roi = king) **Fitz**patrick, **Fitz**gerald

In Spanish families, the children use both the father's name and the mother's name. When a Spanish woman marries, she keeps her own family name and adds her husband's family name. For example, if a woman named **Maria Perez** married a man called **Antonio Chávez**, she would be known as:

Señora Maria **Perez de Chávez** (de = "of, belonging to").

However, the last names of their children would be:

Chávez-Perez

or

Chávez y Perez (y = "and")

Learning About our Names

1. Some first names are very common. Which girls' names are used more than once in your class?

   _____

   _____

2. Which boys' names are used more than once in your class?

   _____

   _____

3. Does someone else in your class have the same first name as you have? If so, how do you feel about it?

   _____

   _____

   _____

   _____

4. Some surnames are long while others are short. Write the surname of *one* person in your class which contains only *one* syllable.

   _____

   _____

5. Write the surname of *two* people in your class who have a *two* syllable surname.

   _____

   _____

6. Repeat with *three* students who have a *three* syllable last name.

   _____

   _____

   _____

7. Find out if your surname has a meaning/history/story. Write it down.

_____

_____

_____

8. Find out if your first name has a meaning/history/story. Write it down.

_____

_____

_____

9. Can you write your first name and/or surname in another language? If so, do it.

_____

_____

_____

10. Can you write anyone else's name in another language? If so, do it.

_____

_____

_____

11. Would you like to see your name written in another language? If so, in which language(s)?

_____

_____

_____

Naming Customs

Today, most people have a first name (forename) and a last name (surname). Many people have one or more middle names. Long ago people had only first names. Most first names were taken from the Bible. In Christian families, children were usually named after saints or ruling kings and queens. In Jewish families, newborn children were often given names of dead grandparents.

Among the Plains Indians of North America, the children's names were usually chosen by older relatives or important leaders. A person did not always keep the same name throughout his life. Young men took a new name after visions of their guardian spirit. Those warriors who performed bravely in battle usually took a new name. If children were sickly, their unlucky names could be thrown away. Sometimes, older men who were near death gave their names to promising young men in the tribe. To receive a name in this way was considered a great honour.

In many Asian and African countries, it is very important to know the day of the week on which a child is born. In Burma, names beginning with certain letters of the alphabet are used to name children born on different days of the week. The day of the week on which a child is born is believed to determine that child's character. For example:

Sunday   - stingy
Monday   - jealous
Tuesday   - honest
Wednesday - cranky
Thursday   - gentle
Friday   - talkative
Saturday   - quarrelsome

The Arkan people of Ghana, a West African country, have a similar naming custom. The Arkan believe that there are seven different ''lifesouls'' — one for each day of the week. Girls born on the same day of the week have the same kind of soul and are given the same name. It is the same for boys.

There are many different naming customs in Canada today. Many families continue to follow their cultural or religious traditions. They name their children after saints, deities, Bible heroes, or respected relatives. Other children are given ''invented names''. Sometimes these names are made up of both parent's names. ''Rayella'' is an invented name. In some families, children are named after famous people, pop stars, movie or television stars. Pet names or nicknames are popular in some families. Other families never use them.

Long ago, using only first names caused confusion, especially when several people had the same name. Gradually, some people were named for their occupation or type of work. Some last names grew out of where people lived or what they looked like. Many last names were based on words for colours or animals.

Questions for Parents and/or Relatives about Naming Customs

1. How are babies' names chosen in our culture/religion?

   _____

   _____

   _____

   _____

2. Is there any special meaning attached to the name(s) given?

   _____

   _____

   _____

   _____

3. Why did you choose to name me _____?
                                        (your name)

   _____

   _____

   _____

   _____

4. Is there any special ceremony associated with baby naming in our culture/religion? If so, describe it.

   _____

   _____

   _____

   _____

   _____

5. Have the naming traditions of our family changed since our family came to Canada? Over the years? If so, describe how.

_____

_____

_____

_____

6. Has our family name ever changed? If so, describe how and why.

_____

_____

_____

_____

How We Can Help

1. List five characteristics you admire in other people.

   _____

   _____

   _____

2. Write a paragraph describing a situation in which you recognized these characteristics in a person/people.

   _____

   _____

   _____

   _____

   _____

   _____

3. Write down the finest compliment you ever received.

   _____

   _____

   _____

4. Why did it make you feel so good?

   _____

   _____

   _____

5. Write down the greatest insult you received.

   _____

   _____

   _____

6. Why did it make you feel so bad?

_____

_____

_____

7. List 5 things you should 'do unto others'.

_____

_____

_____

_____

8. List 5 things you consider 'don't do unto others'.

_____

_____

_____

_____

Teach Me to Fly, Skyfighter

1. Many aspects of being of Chinese origin bothered Sharon. What were some of these?

   _____

   _____

   _____

2. Sharon moved from Vancouver Island to Strathcona. What reasons did she give for not liking her new city?

   _____

   _____

   _____

3. Why was Sharon ashamed of her grandfather?

   _____

   _____

   _____

4. What caused Sharon to begin to accept her Chinese heritage?

   _____

   _____

   _____

5. How did Sharon discriminate? Which people did she discriminate against?

   _____

   _____

   _____

Michi's New Year

1. Why was Michi so unhappy about being a "New Canadian"? Why did she want to return to Japan?

   _____

   _____

   _____

   _____

2. At the beginning of the story, what would have made her happy?

   _____

   _____

   _____

3. Why was New Year important to Michi?

   _____

   _____

   _____

   _____

4. What happened to make her feel happy about her new home?

   _____

   _____

   _____

Calendars and Zodiacs

A calendar is a way of measuring and recording the passage of time. The word "calendar" comes from the Latin word "calendrium" or account book. At one time, a calendar was used to mark the dates when debts had to be paid. Before there were calendars, people measured time by observing natural events. They chose units for sunrise to sunset (day), for moon phases (month) and for the seasons (year). Our Western calendar came from the ancient Babylonian lunar calendar. It was called a lunar calendar because it was based on moons or months. The Babylonian calendar was changed by the ancient Egyptians, Hebrews, Greeks and Romans.

Julius Caesar, the Emperor of Rome, thought that the Roman calendar was not correct, so he made a new one in 46 B.C. The Julian calendar was replaced by the Gregorian calendar. The Gregorian calendar was developed by Pope Gregory in 1580 A.D. It was based on the year of Jesus' birth. Dates before Christ's birth were marked as B.C., which means Before Christ. Dates after the birth of Jesus Christ were marked A.D. A.D. stands for the Latin words "Anno Domini". "Anno Domini" means in the year of our Lord. The Gregorian calendar is used throughout most of the western world today.

There are many different calendars used in Canada. Most people use the Gregorian calendar for everyday things. Canadians of Jewish descent use the ancient Hebrew or Jewish calendar for religious holidays and festivals. The Hebrew calendar is based on the Creation, which was 3760 years and three months before the birth of Christ. The Jewish New Year is called Rosh Hashanah. Rosh Hashanah is celebrated in the Hebrew month of Tishri. Tishri usually corresponds with September on the Gregorian calendar.

Canadians who follow the Muslim religion use the Islamic lunar calendar. It dates from the time Mohammed, the leader of the Muslim religion, fled from his home in the city of Mecca. This happened in 622 A.D. on the Gregorian calendar.

There are many ancient calendars. The Maya, Assyrian, Greek, Roman, Hindu and Chinese people developed their own calendars.

The ancient Chinese lunar calendar was divided into 12 months. Each month lasted 29 or 30 days. Extra months were added to the lunar calendar so it would match the solar year, based on the earth's rotation around the sun.

In ancient times each year was given an animal symbol. People took the animal symbol for the year of their birth as their animal sign. The ancient Chinese believed that a person's animal or zodiac sign told what that person would be like. The animal sign also told what would happen in the person's life. There were 12 animal signs in the Chinese zodiac. People who were born 12 years apart would have the same animal sign. Someone born in 1973, the year of the Ox, would have the same sign as someone born in 1961 or 1985. The ancient Chinese used their zodiac signs to help them decide whom to marry, whom to have for a friend and what business deals to make.

The Chinese Zodiac

In Which Year Were You Born?

Ox (1913, 1925, 1937, 1949, 1961, 1973) You have a calm patient nature. Friends turn to you because you are the rarest of creatures — a good listener.

Tiger (1902, 1914, 1926, 1938, 1950, 1962, 1974) You are a person of extremes. You are both a good friend and a dangerous enemy. You are a deep thinker and a careful planner.

Hare (1903, 1915, 1927, 1939, 1951, 1963, 1975) You are blessed with good fortune. This brings luck at games of chance. You are good at taking care of your money too.

Dragon (1904, 1916, 1928, 1940, 1952, 1964, 1976) On the outside, you are stubborn and quick tempered. But underneath you are really gentle, sensitive and softhearted.

Serpent (1905, 1917, 1929, 1941, 1953, 1965, 1977) You have more than your share of the world's gifts, including wisdom. You are likely to be an attractive, graceful person.

Horse (1906, 1918, 1930, 1942, 1954, 1966, 1978) Your cheerful nature and happy ways make you a popular favourite. Your mental quickness will make you rich and successful.

Ram (1907, 1919, 1931, 1943, 1955, 1967, 1979) You are a sensitive person with considerable talent in all the arts. You will have sucess if you can just put your ability and energy into one activity at a time!

Monkey (1908, 1920, 1932, 1944, 1956, 1968, 1980) You are good at making decisions and handling your money. You are certain to climb to the top and to be a very popular person.

Rooster (1909, 1921, 1933, 1945, 1957, 1969, 1981) With you, it's either all or nothing. You are basically a loner who doesn't trust most people but you have loyal friends.

Dog (1910, 1922, 1934, 1946, 1958, 1970, 1982) You are loyal and honest with a deep sense of duty and justice. You can be trusted to keep secrets.

Boar (1911, 1923, 1935, 1947, 1959, 1971, 1983) You have quiet inner strength and great courtesy. Your energy and ambition will lead you to success.

Rat (1912, 1924, 1936, 1948, 1960, 1972, 1984) You have been blessed with great personal charm and a taste for the good things in life. You have a quick temper but you control it well.

Calendars
Basic Information

Gregorian Calendar

Most people in the western world use the Gregorian calendar. This calendar was established in 1580 by Pope Gregory XIII, but derives its form from the methods of measuring time developed over thousands of years in ancient Babylon, Egypt, Greece and Rome. Its division of the year into 365 days and 12 months beginning with January 1, is based on the movements of the sun. Years are reckoned as B.C. (Before Christ) and A.D. (Anno Domini, in the year of our Lord). Some non-Christians use the designation B.C.E. (Before the Common or Christian Era) and A.C.E. (After the Common or Christian Era) or simply C.E. (Common or Christian Era).

Ecclesiastical Calendar

The calendar used in Christian churches is set according to the movements of both sun and moon. This means that there are certain fixed festivals, such as Christmas, which are always celebrated on the same day of the month every year. The date of others, like Lent and Easter, change from year to year. Many of the festivals have a strong link with pre-Christian observances and worship systems. The traditions of Easter, for example, are connected with a universal concern with the renewal of life in Spring.

Julian Calendar

Called Julian because it was established in the reign of Julius Caesar, this calendar remained in common use throughout the Christian world until the Gregorian calendar was introduced. It divides the year into twelve months of either 30 or 31 days length, resulting in a lag of about 10 days behind the Gregorian system. It remains the calendar of the Eastern Catholic and Orthodox churches and the Coptic church.

Jewish Calendar

According to Jewish tradition, the measurement of time begins with the creation of the world, which took place in the year 3761 B.C.E. The Jewish year begins with Rosh Hashanna (New Year) in autumn. Months are reckoned according to the moon. There are twelve months of alternately 29 and 30 days. A thirteenth month of 29 days is added approximately every three years to keep the calendar in the correct relationship to the seasons.

Islamic Calendar

The Islamic calendar begins with the year Mohammed left Mecca for Medina (622 A.D., according to the Gregorian calendar). It is strictly lunar and, as in Jewish reckoning, there are 12 months of alternately 29 and 30 days a year. Years form a thirty year cycle containing 354 days a year for nineteen years and 355 days a year for the remaining eleven. The most notable difference between the Muslim calendar and others is that it bears no relation to the seasons. Also, festivals do not fall on the same date each year, but vary by about half a month annually.

Hindu Calendar

The Hindu year begins at Baisakhi in April. It is based on lunar reckoning and is divided into twelve months. Every second or third year a month is added to bring it into phase with the solar year. Months begin on fixed dates and are divided into two halves of 15 days each, beginning with the new moon and the full moon. Religious festivals depend on the cycles of the moon and so vary from year to year.

Sikh Calendar

This calendar follows the traditional Indian lunisolar system in determining festivals. The calendar is set annually, using astrological calculations made by authorities at the Sikh temple in Amritsar, India. With the exception of Baisakhi (New Year), which is always celebrated on April 13, all festivals are moveable in relation to the Gregorian calendar.

Aboriginal Calendars

These vary from tribe to tribe, but in all instances are closely related to the movements of nature and the seasons. Every season is considered a special season, a time of thanksgiving to the Creator, the Supreme Spirit and Provider. The sun is an important factor, but at least one group, the Iroquois, reckons the beginning of a new year by the stars.

Chinese Calendar

This calendar originated with a legend in which Buddha commanded all the animals to come to him. When only twelve responded, he named the years in their honour, in the order of their appearance. Chinese New Year falls in January or February, on the first day of the second new moon after winter solstice. Festivals are lunar based. According to Chinese reckoning 1991 represents the year 4688.

Parent/Guardian Questionnaire

In keeping with our overall educational objective of increasing students' knowledge and experiences of the multicultural nature of Canadian society, we shall be undertaking a set of activities designed to expand your child's awareness of the various religious traditions in our midst. So that we may ensure respect for the religions and moral convictions of parents and children involved, we ask that you fill in and sign the following questionnaire.

Name of Parent/Guardian _____

Name of Child _____

Telephone # _____

1. Would you permit your child to take part in guided visits to established religious centers such as churches, temples, synagogues?

   yes ☐   no ☐

2. Would you allow your child to be present, as an observer, at various religious celebrations/festivals?

   yes ☐   no ☐

3. Could you be prepared to visit the class to demonstrate and share your religious celebrations or observances?

   yes ☐   no ☐

4. Would you be prepared to assist in providing the class with contact persons and resources for the above educational activities?

   yes ☐   no ☐

Signature of Parent or Guardian

_____

Date _____

MAJOR RELIGIONS OF THE WORLD

Religion	Origin	Founder	Name for Supreme Being	Symbol	Place of Worship	From of Worship	Sacred Writings	Number of Adherents
BUDDHISM								
CHRISTIANITY								
HINDUISM								
ISLAM								
JUDAISM								

Visiting Places of Worship

1. What is your first impression upon arriving? (eg. simple, ornate, large)

_____

_____

_____

2. Does it remind you of any other place you have visited? If so, in what way(s)?

_____

_____

_____

3. What is the title of the person who leads the service? (eg. rabbi, priest, minister)

_____

_____

_____

4. Is there anything special about the way people enter for a service?

_____

_____

_____

5. Does anyone wear special items of clothing for services? If so, what do they wear?

_____

_____

_____

6. Where do the people sit (or stand) during the service? Do men, women and children sit together?

_____

_____

_____

7. Do you see any holy book? scrolls? Many? A few? Where are they located? What other religious items do you see?

_____

_____

_____

_____

8. Look around you. Ask your guide to explain the significance of any features that you have never seen before. What have you learned?

_____

_____

_____

9. Does this "feel" like a holy place? Explain your answer.

_____

_____

_____

10. How did you feel as you left? Was it the same as how you felt when you entered?

_____

_____

_____

11. Look around again as you are leaving. If you wanted to visit a similar place of worship, how would you be able to recognize it? What features would you look for on the outside?

_____

_____

_____

12. Draw a sketch of some of the things you saw during your visit, or describe in writing an item which made a strong impression on you.

_____

_____

_____

Case Study: Prejudice and Discrimination

Mei Ling was a friendly 10 year old girl who was in fifth grade at _____.
Your school

Mei Ling was an only child who was born in Montreal. Her parents were born in China and emigrated to Canada twelve years ago.

One day, on her way home from school, Mei Ling and two of her friends stopped in at the corner candy store to buy some licorice.

As soon as they entered, Mr. Taylor, the owner of the candy store, pointed an accusing finger at Mei Ling. He then said, "How can you have the nerve to come back in here after you stole some chocolate bars from me last week?" Mei Ling's first reaction was one of shock! She had never stolen anything in her life. She broke into tears and looked at the floor, too embarrased to face Cheryl and Linda. Linda put her arms around her, to try and console her, while Cheryl politely but firmly said to the owner, "You are definitely mistaken. Mei Ling has been our friend since grade one. She would never take anything that doesn't belong to her. Mr. Taylor you owe her an apology".

"Get out of my store and never come back! I told you that last week and I'm repeating it now. You're lucky I'm not calling the police!" Mr. Taylor said.

The girls left the store and after a while Mei Ling's friends were able to calm her enough to stop her sobbing. They discussed the incident and tried to figure out why Mr. Taylor blamed Mei Ling for stealing. When Mei Ling regained her composure, and was able to think clearly, she addressed her friends, "I've figured it out. Can you?"

Her friends still puzzled said, "Please explain it to us. We still don't understand". Mei Ling responded, "Look at me and then look at each other. Can't you see the difference?"

"You mean its because you're Chinese?" asked Cheryl. "What does that have to do with it?" asked Linda.

"To Mr. Taylor, all Chinese people look alike," answered Mei Ling.

"That's ridiculous all three of us look different from each other," said Cheryl.

Books

FICTION

Allison, Rosemary. *The Pillow*. Toronto: Lorimer, 1979.
Angelina, newly arrived from Italy, is teased by schoolmates because she cannot speak English. Her friend Ram, whose family has immigrated from India, helps her to adjust to Canadian life.
(S)

Andrews, Jan. (editor). *The Dancing Sun*. Victoria: Porcepic Press, 1981.
Stories and poems of Canadian children from different ethnic backgrounds.
(S)

Archer, Colleen. *Foxy and the Missing Mask*. Kapuskasing: Penumbra, 1986.
Mark Crowe, a fourteen year-old Kwakiutl, searches for Foxy, his retriever dog, and for the rare mask carved by his father.
(S)

Brown, Richard. *Storyworlds I and II*. London: Oliver and Boyd, 1990.
These multicultural collections of traditional and contemporary literature include myths, legends, folk tales, fables, poems, short stories and extracts from novels and plays. Teachers' guide available.
(S)

Coerr, Eleanor. *Sadako and the Thousand Paper Cranes*. New York: Dell Publishing, 1990.
The story of a young Japanese girl who gets arlétis, leukaemia as a result of radiation from the atomic bomb dropped on Hiroshima.
(S)

Craig, John. *Who Wants to be Alone?* Richmond Hill: Scholastic, 1972.
Eighteen year-old Zach leaves the Ontario Ojibway reserve where he grew up to look for traces of his own tribe, the Agawa. He links up with others who are looking for a place to belong. His pilgrimage across the continent raises thought-provoking questions about values.
(S)

Doyle, Brian. *Angel Square*. Toronto: Groundwood Books, 1990.
Tommy, who lives in Ottawa, just after World War II, takes his life in his hands each day as he crosses Angel Square. His route used by hostile children from different religious groups, fighting to get to their schools. When the father of Tommy's Jewish friend Sammy is beaten up, Tommy is determined to find out who is responsible.
(S)

D'Olyey, Enid. *Between Sea and Sky*. Stratford: William-Wallace, 1979.
Two young black girls from Canada take a holiday with their parents in Jamaica, where they begin the process of finding out about their roots.
(S)

Duncan, Francis. *Kap-Sung Ferris*. Toronto: MacMillan, 1977.
Kap-Sung is a teenage Korean girl raised from babyhood by her adoptive Canadian family. When confronted with prejudice, she wonders if she really belongs in Canada, and stows away on a ship bound for Korea to seek her own identity. (S)

Elston, Georgia. *Giving: Ojibwa Stories and Legends from the Children of Curve Lake*. Lakefield: Waapone, 1985.
School children gathered to retell and illustrate the stories which they had heard from their elders. (S)

Greene, Betty. *Summer of my German Soldier*. New York: Bantam Books, 1984.
The powerful story of a twelve-year old Jewish girl who hides an escaped German prisoner of war in a racist Arkansas town during World War II. (S)

Hancock, Lyn, with Marion Dowler. *Tell Me, Grand-Mother*. Toronto: McClelland and Stewart, 1985.
Jane, a Métis, tells the tales of her life to her grandson, Dennis. Married to Sam Livingstone, she lived through exciting times in the West during the 19th century.
(S)

Heneghan, Jim. *Promises to Come*. Markham: Grolier Ltd., 1988.
Becky is upset and hostile when the Vietnamese "baby" her parents are sponsoring turns out to be a teenager older than she is. Kim, haunted by memories of her experiences in Vietnam and the refugee camps, tries to come to terms with her past, before she can begin a new life in Canada. (S)

Holman, Felice. *The Wild Children*. Markham: Penguin Books, 1983.
Left behind when his family is arrested by soldiers during the dark days following the Bolshevik revolution, twelve year-old Alex falls in with a gang of other desperate homeless children, but never loses hope for a better life.
(S)

Hughes, Monica. *Log Jam*. Toronto: Irwin Publishing Company, 1987.
Isaac Manyfeathers, a Native boy who has escaped from a detention centre, and Lenora Rydz, a non-Native, fleeing a difficult family situation, meet in the rugged Alberta foothills and help to free each other from personal prisons. The stories of Isaac's grandmother become "a pattern for going forward."
(S)

Jacobs, Joseph. *Indian Fairy Tales*. Toronto: General Publishing, 1969.
Twenty-nine traditional tales from India, including some of the oldest recorded tales.
(S/T)

Kleitsch, Christel and Paul Stevens. *Dancing Feathers*. Toronto: Annick Press, 1988.
Taria, a young Ojibway girl from Spirit Bay in northern Canada, begins to understand the importance of her heritage when she takes part in her first Pow Wow. (S)

Kogawa, Joy. *Naomi's Road*. Toronto: Oxford University Press, 1986.
The story of Naomi Nakane, a little girl with "black hair and lovely Japanese eyes and a face like a valentine" and her Japanese-Canadian family during the 1940's, when Canada was at war with Japan. (S)

Kong, Shiu L. and Elizabeth Wong. *Fables and Legends from Ancient China*. Toronto: Kensington Educational, 1985.
Folktales from ancient China. (S)

Konigsburg, E.L. *About the B'Nai Bagels*. New York: Yearling Books, Dell Publishing Company, 1990.
Mark Setzer thought he had enough aggravation studying for his Bar Mitzvah and losing his best friend. It's the last straw when his mother becomes the new manager of his Little League baseball team and drags his older brother along as the coach. (S)

Lim, Sing. *West Coast Chinese Boy*. Montreal: Tundra Books, 1979.
An illustrated portrayal of the life of the Chinese community in Vancouver, early in this century. The author draws on his own past, recalling the daily details, the joys and hardships, the times of celebrations and the external hostility he experienced as a boy. (S)

Little, Jean. *From Anna*. New York: Harper and Row Publishers, 1972.
Anna's family leaves Germany in 1933 when the Nazi government begins its repressive regime. Life in Canada is not easy for Anna, who has always been clumsy and "different". When her correctable disability is diagnosed, Anna's world changes. (S)

Little, Jean. *Kate*. Scarborough, Ontario: Harper Collins, 1973.
Kate's father is Jewish, her mother is not. What is Kate? An intriguing pre-teen novel about Kate's search for answers. (S)

Matas, Carol. *Lisa*. Toronto: Lester and Orpen Dennys Publications, 1987.
A hard hitting story about the strength and courage of the Danish resistance to the Nazi invasion during World War II, told through the eyes of a teenaged girl who helped Danish Jews escape the Holocaust. (S)

Mehta, Lila. *Enchanted Anklet*. Toronto: Lilmur Publications, 1985.
The East Indian version of the Cinderella story, translated and adapted by Lila Mehta. (S)

North American Indian Travelling College. *Legends of our Nations*. Cornwall Island, Ontario, 1984.
Best-loved stories which teach native values, selected from across Canada. (S)

Nowlan, Alden. *Nine Micmac Legends*. Hantsport, Nova Scotia: Lancelot Press, 1983.
Stories that teach values which are relevant to today's children and grown-ups alike, illustrated by Shirley Bear. (S)

Pasternak, Carol and Allen Sutterfield. *Stone Soup*. Toronto: Women's Press, 1974.
A group of children is tricked into a new awareness of other cultures when they make "stone soup". A retelling of a traditional tale. (S)

Sadiq, Nazneen. *Camels Can Make You Homesick and Other Stories*. Toronto: James Lorimer, 1985.
In these entertaining stories, five children, in five different places, cope with the challenge of growing up both Canadian and South-Asian. (S)

San Souci, Robert D. *The Enchanted Tapestry*. Toronto: Groundwood Books, 1987.
A traditional Chinese tale of the magnificent tapestry woven by the mother of three sons, only the youngest of whom is truly devoted to her. (S)

Schwartz, Ellen. *Starshine*. Vancouver: Polestar, 1987.
Starshine Bliss Shapiro has had a hard time coming to terms with her family's alternative life style. This changes when she becomes friends with Julie Wong, a Chinese-Canadian recently arrived from Hong Kong. Star is happy to discover that there are other kids who eat tofu and are interested in challenging hobbies. (S)

Shevrin, Aliza. *Holiday Tales of Sholom Aleichem*. New York: MacMillan Publishers, 1985.
Seven stories, each revolving around the celebration of a Jewish holiday. (S/T)

Smucker, Barbara. *Days of Terror*. Toronto: Penguin Books, 1981. The story of a Mennonite family's struggle for survival during and after the Russian revolution, and their ultimate emigration to Canada. (S)

Smucker, Barbara. *Underground to Canada*. Toronto: Penguin Books, 1978.
While Jubilly slaved on the brutal cotton plantation, she dreamed of running away to the distant northern land called Canada, where all people could be free. In the end, she did more than dream. (S)

Steptoe, John. *Mufaro's Beautiful Daughter. An African Tale.* New York: Lothrop, Lee and Sheppard Books, 1987.
When the King decided to take a wife, he invited the most worthy and beautiful daughters in the land to come before him. Mufaro declared proudly that only the King could choose between his two beautiful daughters. (S)

Strickland, Dorothy S. (editor). *Listen Children. An Anthology of Black Literature.* New York: Bantam Books, 1986.
A collection of stories, poems and experiences by many of the most gifted black writers. While the book is addressed to black children who are learning about their heritage, all children will learn to value themselves and others as they read through this anthology. (S)

Tanaka, Shelley. *Michi's New Year.* Toronto: Northern Lights, 1980.
Michi celebrates Japanese New Year in Canada.

Tehanetorens. *Tales of the Iroquois. Volume I.* Ohsweken, Ontario: Iroqrafts, 1976.
The story "Gift of the Great Spirit" is excellent for dramatizing and teaching the value of caring for others. (S)

Wallace, Ian and Angela Wood. *The Sandwich.* Toronto: Kids Can Press, 1975.
When Vincenzo produces a "stinky meat and cheese sandwich", the children in his class are appalled. As the story progresses, they learn to accept his sandwich, while Vincenzo learns that understanding a different culture is a gradual process. (S)

Walter, Mildred Pitts. *Brother to the Wind.* New York: Lothrop, Lee and Sheppard Books, 1985.
With the help of Good Snake, a young African boy gets his dearest wish. (S)

Wartski, Maureen Crane. *A Boat to Nowhere.* New York: Westminster Press, 1980.
The story of three Vietnamese children and their grandfather who leave the dangers of their village to become "boat people", searching for freedom in another country. (S)

Weir, Joan. *So, I'm Different.* Vancouver: Douglas & McIntyre, 1981.
A gripping, contemporary story about a boy who is the only Indian in his school. Includes native legends. (S)

Yee, Paul. *Tales from the Gold Mountain.* Toronto: Groundwood Books, 1989.
Eight short stories which combine the rough and tumble adventure of frontier life with the rich bolk traditions of Chinese immigrants. (S)

Yee, Paul. *Teach Me to Fly, Skyfighter and other Stories.* Toronto: James Lorimer and Company, 1983.
Kites, Kung-fu and soccer engage four active Chinese-Canadian children growing up in a downtown neighbourhood near Vancouver's Chinatown. (S)

Yee, Paul. *The Curses of Third Uncle.* Toronto: James Lorimer and Company, 1986.
A tale of intrigue, adventure and betrayal, set in Vancouver in the early 1900's. Above all, it is the story of one girl's fiery determination to find out the truth and save her family. (S)

Yerou, Aristides and Cathleen Hoskins. *The Friendship Solution.* Toronto: James Lorimer and Company, 1984.
Aleka has moved to a new neighbourhood, and is having trouble making friends. Will she take the "test" of friendship and steal a piece of her mother's jewelry? (S)

Yu, Chai-Shin, Shiu L. Kong and Ruth W. Yu. *Korean Folk Tales.* Toronto: Kensington Educational, 1986.
The spiritual beliefs and the distinctive culture of the Korean people are captured in this attractive collection of ancient Korean tales. (S)

NON-FICTION

Abello, Chana Byers. *The Children We Remember.* Rockville, Maryland: Kar-Ben Copies Inc., 1983.
An illustrated history of children and events surrounding the Holocaust. (S/T)

Benedict, Rebecca and Charis Wahl. *St. Regis Reserve.* Toronto: Fitzhenry & Whiteside, 1976.
A glimpse of children's lives on the St. Regis (also known as Akwesasne) reserve today. Many photographs, although not of high quality. (S/T)

Breon, Robin and Vera Cudjoe. *The Story of Mary Ann Shadd.* Toronto: Carib-Can, 1988.
A short, easy-to-read introduction to the life of this inspirational and important figure in black history in Canada. (S)

Bull, Angela. *Anne Frank — Profiles.* London: Hamish Hamilton Children's Books, 1984.
The story of Anne Frank, a young Jewish girl living in Holland during the second World War, who spent 2 years in hiding with her family. During that period, she kept a diary which her father, the only family member to survive the Holocaust, discovered when he returned to their hiding place after the war. (S/T)

Chaiken, M. *Light Another Candle: The Story and*

Meaning of Hanukha. New York: Clarion, 1981.
A clearly written, attractively illustrated book about Hanukah and the holiday customs, with a useful glossary, historical chronology, and bibliography.
(S)

Frank, Anne. *Anne Frank. The Diary of a Young Girl.* New York: Doubleday and Company, 1967.
Born in Germany in 1929, Anne Frank spent the last two years of her life hidden in a nest of rooms in Amsterdam, during the Nazi occupation. She describes her experiences and confides her young adolescent feelings in her diary.
(S)

Fritz, Jean. *Homesick. My Own Story.* Toronto: Dell Publishing Company, 1990.
Jean Fritz was born in China and lived there until 1927, when she was twelve. Her parents' memories of home, and letters from relatives in Pennsylvania made her identity strongly as an American, and homesick for a place that she had never seen.
(S)

Greenwood, Barbara and Audrey McKim. *My Special Vision.* Toronto: Irwin Publishing, 1987.
The biography of Jean Little, award-winning children's author. Born almost totally blind, she spent her early years in Taiwan, where her parents worked as military missionaries.
(S)

Kurelek, William and Margaret S. Engelhart. *They Sought a New World! The Story of European Immigration to North America.* Montreal: Tundra Books, 1988.
Margaret Engelhart has put together an excellent selection of William Kurelek's striking paintings and his own words on the experience of European settlement in Canada. (S/T)

Little, Jean. *Little by Little.* Markham, Ontario: Penguin Books Canada Ltd., 1987.
Nearly blind from birth, Jean Little has led an extraordinary life. Subjected to ridicule, rejection and bullying, she withdrew into a world of her own. An honest, moving, and sometimes funny autobiography which describes the joys and pains of childhood and growing up, of family, of love and of being different.
(S)

Ortiz, Simon. *The People Shall Continue.* New York: Children's Book Press, 1988.
The epic story of the survival of the aboriginal people, from creation to the present, told in the rhythmic cadences of a Native American poet.
(S/T)

Petry, Ann. *Harriet Tubman, Conductor of the Underground Railway.* New York: Archway, 1971.
The story of Harriet Tubman, a woman called Moses, who set her people free.
(S)

Preusch, Deb, Tom Barry and Beth Wood. *Red Ribbons for Emma.* New Seed, 1981.
Winner of Akwesasne Notes' Children's Book Award for presenting "the truth about our peoples' struggles to survive."
(S)

Reiss, Johanna. *The Upstairs Room.* New York: Harper and Row, 1987.
The room in the title of this autobiography was the hiding place for Johanna and her sister in the home of a non-Jewish family in war torn Holland in the 1940's.
(S)

Sawyer, Don. *Where the Rivers Meet.* Winnipeg: Pemmican, 1989.
After the suicide of a friend, Nancy Antoine, a young Shushwap high school student in a small B.C. town, discovers how traditional spiritual ways can meet modern problems. We come to understand both the frustration and pain and the spiritual strength and hope of young aboriginal people today.
(S)

Segal, Lore. *Other People's Houses.* Toronto: Random House of Canada, 1986.
In December, 1983, nine months after Hitler took over Austria, six hundred Austrian children were evacuated by train to England. Ten year old Lore Graszmann Segal was one of them.
(S)

Sterling, Dorothy. *Freedom Train.* Toronto: Scholastic Inc., 1954.
Born into slavery, young Harriet Tubman knew only hard work and hunger. When she finally escaped north by a secret route known as the Underground Railway, she did not forget her people.
(S)

Takashima, Shizuye. *A Child in a Prison Camp.* Montreal: Tundra, 1984.
With sensitivity and no rancour, the artist recalls her childhood in a Japanese prison camp in the Canadian Rockies during World War II.
(S)

Vineberg, Esther. *Grandmother Came From Dwortz.* Montreal: Tundra, 1984.
A Jewish family leaves Czarist Russia and immigrates first to New York and then to New Brunswick, at the turn of the century.
(S)

Charts, Games, and Kits

Family Treasures. Hull, Quebec: Canadian Museum of Civilization.
A hands-on, multicultural, cross-curriculum activity kit which enables students to explore their roots through researching family treasures, such as artifacts, paintings, letters.
(S)

Multicultural Docupack. Toronto: J.M. Dent and Sons, 1980.
A package of illustrative materials documenting the multicultural nature of Canadian society. It contains more than two hundred items, including documents, photographs, posters, collages, maps, display materials and booklets focusing on the major themes that highlight our multicultural experience. (S/T)

Pictorial Charts Educational Trust. Toronto: Can.-Ed. Media Ltd., 1989
1. Birth Rites
2. Buddhist Festivals
3. Hindu Festivals
4. Initiation Rites
5. Islamic Festivals
6. Jewish Festivals
7. Marriage Rites
8. Sikh Festivals
Pictorial charts with teachers' guides, depicting various religions, festivals and rites. (S/T)

Pictorial Wallcharts. Toronto: Far Eastern Books, 1989.
1. My Neighbours Religion
2. Acts of Worship
3. Places of Worship
4. Days of Worship
5. Religious Artifacts
6. Jewish Festivals
7. Islamic Festivals
8. Hindu Festivals
9. Buddhist Festivals
10. Sikh Festivals
11. Chinese Festivals
12. Birth Rites
13. Initiation Rites
14. Marriage Rites
15. Wealth Rites
16. Creation Stories I
17. Creation Stories II
18. Ways of Seeing
19. Holy Writings
20. Holy Books I
21. Holy Books II
22. Sharing the World
23. Founders and Messengers
24. Religion in Art I
25. Religion in Art II
26. Religion in Art III
27. Hindu Gods
28. Hindu Places
Full colour pictorial wall charts with teachers' notes. (S/T)

Shirts, R. Garry. *Rafa Rafa.* Delmar, California: Simile II, 1976.
A cross cultural simulation game. (S/T)

The Alberta People Kit. Edmonton, Alberta: The Alberta Multicultural Commission, 1984.
A unique multi-medi cultural heritage awareness education kit developed primarily for use in upper elementary classes. The video and print materials in the kit are an indispensable resource for teachers and students involved in the integration of multicultural activities in various subject areas. Although some materials are specific to Alberta's multicultural heritage, most are appropriate for general use. (S/T)

Together We're Better. Ottawa: Department of the Secretary of State. Multiculturalism and Citizenship. 1989.
This resource package includes: a resources guide for use in the school and community with suggestions for initiatives and activities to help eliminate racial discrimination; background information on racism in Canada; a poster, stickers and buttons to promote the theme "Together We're Better".
(S/T)

Films and Videos

Charlie Squash Goes to Town. Montreal: National Film Board of Canada, 1969.
This amusing, penetrating story focuses on the ironies involved in trying to remain Indian in a non-Indian world. Whimsical drawings of memorable incidents illustrate cultural confusion.
Film time: 4 min. 26 sec. 16 MM (S)

Gurdeep Singh Bains. Montreal: National Film Board of Canada, 1976. Series: Children of Canada.
Gurdeep is a thirteen-year-old baptized Canadian Sikh whose family runs a dairy farm near Chilliwack, B.C. The family has retained their language, religion and cultural practices. Gurdeep's well integrated life includes attending the Sikh temple, playing soccer with his friends and working on the farm. Yet, sometimes, he feels different from other children. Support material available.
Film time: 11 min. 55. sec. 16MM (S)

Overture: Linh from Viet Nam. Toronto: Marlin Distributors, 1980.
Linh Tran, who has immigrated from Vietnam, and her neighbour, Jose Agular, a Mexican-American, become friends when they discover their mutual interest in music and their shared talent for playing the flute. Their friendship is threatened when Linh wins the place in the school band that Jose had been counting on. When Linh's flute is stolen, she is sure that Jose has taken it. Using money that he has saved for a tape deck, Jose retrieves the flute. The two friends are reunited in a duet; a

symbol of their strengthened friendship.
Film time: 26 mins. 16MM (S)

My Name is Susan Yee. Montreal: National Film Board of Canada, 1975. Series: Children of Canada.
A perceptive, outspoken view of downtown Montreal through the eyes of Susan Yee, a young Chinese-Canadian. At home, at school, at play on Mount Royal, Susan picks up on adult foibles and provides an enlightened, amusing perspective on the city.
Film time: 12 min. 18 sec. 16 MM and VHS (S)

Strangers at the Door. Montreal: National Film Board of Canada, 1977.
This story, which takes place aboard an immigrant ship and in an immigration shed, shows the experiences of the Laluki family as they enter Canada. Viewers observe the family's bewilderment at the questions asked by immigration officials and the heartbreak when their daughter is not allowed to enter.
Film time: 28 min. 16 MM and VHS (S)

Teach Me to Dance. Montreal: National Film Board of Canada, 1978.
Lesia convinces her English-Canadian friend Sarah to perform a Ukrainian dance with her as part of the school's Christmas pageant. But Sarah's father, angry at the growing number of Ukrainian settlers in his community, forbids Sarah to participate with Lesia. The girls retain their strong friendship, despite the prejudices of their parents, and celebrate Christmas day together in Sarah's barn, where they dance. Support material available.
Film time: 28 mins. 35 secs. 16 MM and VHS (S)

The Bamboo Brush. Toronto: Atlantic Films, 1983.
A film adaptation of Adele La Rouche's book *Binky and the Bamboo Brush*. Benjamin disappoints his father by sneaking out of his Chinese language class to play video games. Confined to home, Benjy learns the art of observation from his grandfather, a meticulous Chinese painter. The young boy becomes a skilled artist and grows very close to his grandfather. When his grandfather dies, Benjy finds new abilities and qualities in himself which mark his passage from childhood to maturity.
Film time: 25 mins. 16MM and VHS (S)

The House at 12 Rose Street. Toronto: Marlin Distributors, 1980.
When the first black family in the neighbourhood moves in next door to fourteen year-old Bobby Miller, he is confronted by evidence of racial prejudice on the part of his neighbours. Bobby finds himself caught between his growing friendship with his new neighbour, Will Franklin, and loyalty to his buddy, Jack Barrett, who has repeatedly demonstrated bigotry towards blacks. After many incidents of prejudice against the Franklins, Bobby learns that ignoring injustices is the same as condoning them.
Film time: 32 mins. 16MM (S)

The New Canadian Kid. Toronto: Kinetic, 1980.
This video, in the form of a children's drama, enacts the difficulties encountered by a non-English speaking immigrant child and his family.
Video time: 40 mins. (S)

Veronica. Montreal: National Film Board of Canada, 1977. Series: Children of Canada.
Nine year-old Veronica Makarewicz performs Polish dances, goes to Polish school twice a week and talks to Polish customers in her parents' bakery. But, as this film shows, she is also very Canadian.
Film time: 14 mins. 13 sec. 16 MM (S)

Filmstrips and Audio Cassettes

Black Fugitive. Montreal: National Film Board of Canada, 1979.
This sound filmstrips begins with a description of the slave trade and then follows the adventures of a small group of slaves who fled the United States via the Underground Railway to freedom in Canada. (S)

Celebrating Together. Montreal: National Film Board of Canada, 1985.
Two filmstrips: *The Prophet* focuses on Jews celebrating Passover and *Jump-Up* describes Caribbean groups rejoicing at carnival time. (S)

Childhood Memories of a Japanese-Canadian — Lost Years. Montreal: National Film Board of Canada and the National Museum of Man, 1980.
This filmstrip presents a Japanese Canadian family's experiences through the turbulent war years, vividly recreating the drama of the evacuation, the heartache and uncertainty of leaving home and the routine of daily life in a detention camp. (S)

Josiah Henson: A Remarkable Black Canadian. Montreal: National Film Board of Canada, 1979. Series: The History of Blacks in Canada.
This filmstrip recounts the story of Josiah Henson, a man of remarkable courage and understanding. A black slave, he escaped to freedom in Upper Canada. He has been identified as the hero of *Uncle Tom's Cabin*. (S)

Lennon, John. *Imagine*. From *Imagine*, Capitol Records. Available on record, cassette and CD.

Making Faces. The Culture Behind the Mask.
Montreal: National Film Board of Canada, 1988.
Masks are found in every civilization and they
share common traits in widely diverse cultures.
This filmstrip and cassette explore the traditional
forms of masks, dances, art and drama found in
Canadian communities. The teacher's guide
includes follow-up activities in many subject areas.
Also available on video. (S)

Not So Different. Montreal: National Film Board of
Canada, 1984.
A humorous tale of a land where everyone and
everything was the same. Then, one day, very
different strangers arrived. An excellent discussion
starter in today's multicultural classroom. Also
available on video. (S)

Stevens, Ray. *Everything is Beautiful.* From *Ray
Steven's Greatest Hits.* M.C.A. Available on record
and cassette.

West Coast Chinese Boy. Montreal: National Film
Board of Canada, 1987.
In this autobiographical filmstrip, an old Chinese
man looks back on his father's arrival in Canada
and his own childhood. We see some humorous
situations and incidents in Sing Lim's school,
home and community life. But we also learn how
he was looked down on by various Canadians,
including members of the older Chinese community, and how he dealt with prejudice from
"white" children. (S)

Reference Books and Other Publications

Bowers, Vivien and Diane Swanson. *Exploring
Canada. Learning from the Past, Looking to the Future.*
Toronto: Nelson Canada, 1989.
An examination of Canada and Canadians, in the
past and present. In the unit dealing with immi-
gration, we learn about the challenges newcomers
face and the contributions they make to Canada.
(S/T)

Browder, Sue. *The New Age Baby Book.* New York:
Warner Books, 1987.
The chapter titled "Choosing a Name that Reflects
our Roots" provides an overview of names collected from various cultures, and describes the
traditions, customs and naming practices associated
with each culture. (S/T)

Bruce, Jean. *After the War.* Toronto: Fitzhenry and
Whiteside, 1982.
Jean Bruce, herself an immigrant, uses hundreds of
in-depth interviews from across Canada to tell the
stories of immigrants who fulfilled their dreams
and dispelled the fears of others while establishing
new roots. She ranged the country to find photographs in churches, ethnic organizations, private
albums, the Public Archives, and diverse libraries
and museums. (T)

Canada's Ethnic Groups Series. Ottawa: Canadian
Historical Association, 1982.
A series of booklets containing concise histories of
Canada's ethno-cultural groups. Each account
traces the origins, development and contemporary
situation of the group within Canada. The follow-
ing histories are currently available in English and
French: the Chinese, East Indians, Finns,
Germans, Japanese, Jews, Poles, Portuguese,
Scots, Ukrainians and West Indians. (T)

*The Canadian Charter of Rights and Freedoms.
Teachers' Manual and a Guide for Students.* Ottawa:
Department of the Secretary of State. Multicultural-
ism and Citizenship, 1985.
An excellent basic resource for teachers and secon-
dary school students which enhances understand-
ing of the nature and implications of the charter.
(S/T)

The Canadian Citizen. Ottawa: Department of the
Secretary of State. Multiculturalism and
Citizenship, 1985.
A thorough outline of the rights, privileges and
responsibilities of Canadian citizenship. (T)

The Canadian Enclyclopedia (Volumes I-IV).
Edmonton: Hurtig Publishers, 1988.
This comprehensive encyclopedia includes useful
entries on Canada's ethnic and racial diversity.
(S/T)

Carter, Velma and Levero Carter. *The Black
Canadians, their History and Contributions.*
Edmonton: Reidmore Books, 1989.
An excellent teacher reference and resource that
deals with the history of black Canadians from
early settlement to the present, in various regions
of the country. In addition to describing events
and personalities in black Canadian history, the
text presents case studies which can be used to
teach about racism in Canada, human rights and
other related isues. (T)

Couner, Daniel C.G. and Doreen Bethune Johnson. *Native People and Explorers of Canada.* Toronto:
Prentice Hall Canada, 1984.
A description of native life and the stories of
individual native people, written from the perspective of two native children, one living in Copper-
mine on the Arctic coast, the other living on the
Capilano Reserve on the Pacific coast. Also
included are descriptions of the contacts between
European explorers such as Jacques Cartier, Henry

lsey and James Cook and native people.   (S/T)

mentary School Curriculum Guides (levels IV-VI): ral and Religious Education. Quebec: Ministry of ucation, Government of Quebec, 1986.
eful guidelines for teachers working in multicul- al and multi-religious education. The objectives d activities under Module Two, ''Celebrations'' d those under Module Three, ''Relationships'' of special interest to teachers working in a lticultural school and community.   (T)

unfeld, Frederic V. Games of the World Geneva: IICEF.
encyclopedic volume celebrating the history d evolution of more than 100 games around the rld, featuring excellent photographs, lively text d details directions for making and playing nes.   (S/T)

cker, Carlotta. The Book of Canadians. Edmonton: rtig Publishers, 1983.
lendidly illustrated and presented in a lively and ry readable style, this is the first dictionary of nadian biography written especially for young ople. With more than 700 entries, spanning nost 1000 years, it is packed with a fascinating ay of characters, including a wide selection of iievers who are not featured in most reference oks. Includes prominent Canadians of different ino-cultural origins.   (S/T)

dian and Northern Affairs Canada. Indians and Inuit Canada and The Canadian Indian. Ottawa: Ministry Supply and Services Canada, 1990 and 1986.
ese two, short government publications provide ormation about the history of the First Peoples, eir origins and cultures and their aspirations.   (T)

inston, Basil. Ojibway Ceremonies. Toronto: :Clelland & Stewart, 1983.
ese stories, told in legend form, deal with Ojib- iy spirituality.   (T)

inston, Basil. Ojibway Heritage. Toronto: :Clelland & Stewart, 1979.
guide to understanding traditional Ojibway nbols and values.   (T)

lman, Bobby. The Crabtree Countries and Festivals the World Series. Toronto: Crabtree Publishing mpany, 1982.
series of 16 booklets (2 per country) cover the lowing countries or regions: Greece, Hong ng, India, Italy, Japan, Portugal, West Germany d the Caribbean.   (S)

estig-Tobias, Lenore. Resources Reading List 1990. nadian Alliance in Solidarity with the Native oples, P.O. Box 574, Station P, Toronto, Ontario 5S 2T1, 1990.

An excellent annotated bibliography of resources by and about native people in Canada and the United States, which includes listings of print and visual curriculum material for children and for elementary schools. A must for teachers focusing on native studies.   (T)

Kehoe, John. A Handbook for Enhancing the Multi- cultural Climate of the School. Vancouver: Western Education Development Group, 1984.
This handbook is designed to help children to become citizens in a multicultural society. It covers topics such as: how to assess the multicultural needs of a school; methods of evaluating and developing curriculum; ways of changing attitudes; and background material on cultural practices. An excellent general teacher reference to set the con- text for multiculturalism in education, as well as a useful reference for all subject areas.   (T)

Krause, Marina. Multicultural Mathematics Material. Virginia: The National Council of Teachers of Mathematics Inc., 1983.
Activities and games collected from around the world, which bring the vitality of ethnic and cul- tural diversity to mathematics.   (T)

Le Centre Interculturel Monchanin. The Persistence of Native Indian Values. Montreal, 1984.
Articles and book reviews, in English and French.   (T)

Mayled, Jon. Religious Festivals. London: Wayland Publishers Ltd., 1987.
Each chapter looks at the religious celebrations and festivals of one of the following religions — Judaism, Christianity, Hinduism, Islam, Buddhism and Sikhism. Beautiful photographs help to bring these festivals to life.   (S/T)

Multiculturalism in Canada. A Graphic Overview. Ottawa: Policy and Research, Department of Multi- culturalism and Citizenship, 1989.
This report presents a graphic overview of Canada's ethnic, racial and linguistic diversity. A series of charts and statistical information deal with ethnic origin, language, immigration, visible minorities and aboriginal people in Canada, the provinces and territories. Information is based primarily on data from the 1986 census.   (T)

Multiculturalizing. A Series of Resource Guides for Educators. Ottawa: Department of the Secretary of State. Multiculturalism and Citizenship, 1987.
A series of booklets which provide teachers with valuable resource lists and suggestions on how to incorporate multiculturalism into the teaching of all subject areas. The series currently includes: Educa- tional through Children's Literature; Multiculturalism Education through Art; Multiculturalizing Parent

Involvement; and *Play, Physical Education and Recreation.* (T)

Multifaith Calendar. Canadian Ecumenical Action, 1410 West 12th Avenue, Vancouver, B.C. V6H 1M8.
A calendar which identifies the religious celebrations and significant events of the major religious and spiritual traditions. It also provides explanatory notes on the calendar systems of the different religions. (S/T)

Musical Instruments of the World. New York: UNICEF, 1976.
More than 4000 original drawings are used to classify and explain hundreds of instruments, past and present. (T)

North American Travelling College. *Traditional Teachings.* Cornwall Island, Ontario, 1984.
The way of life and culture of the Iroquois peoples, from the oral traditions, interpreted by their Elders and teachers. Written for the young, but of interest to everyone. (S/T)

Paper, Jordan. *Offering Smoke: The Sacred Pipe and Native American Religion.* Edmonton: University of Alberta Press, 1988.
The history, mythology, ritual and symbolism of the ancient pipe are studied "with careful regard for the religious and cultural sensitivites so vital for genuine understanding". The book includes 60 colour photos of pipes. Royalties go to the St. Charles Community (Ojibway). (T)

Parry, Caroline. *Let's Celebrate.* Toronto: Kids Can Press, 1987.
A comprehensive introduction to all of the holidays celebrated by the many cultural communities in Canada. (S/T)

Polon, Linda and Aileen Cantwell. *The Whole Earth Holiday Book.* Chicago: Scott, Foresman and Company, 1983.
The religious and secular celebrations and festivals of people around the world are arranged by season. A variety of activities follow each description. In some cases, a festival is described in general terms, and we learn how it is celebrated by people in countries around the world. (S/T)

Religions on the World Series. London: Wayland Publishers Ltd., 1986.
Six books covering the following religious traditions: Buddhism, Christianity, Hinduism, Islam, Judaism and Sikhism. Each book is beautifully illustrated and outlines the history of each religion, including important customs and festivals. (S/T)

Religious Stories Series. London: Wayland Publishers Ltd., 1986.

Ten books which contain stories for children from the major religious traditions. The stories will help children see the relationship between their religious and/or cultural group and other cultures and religions. The books are beautifully illustrated in the traditional style of each religion. Titles in the series are: *Buddhist Stories; Chinese Stories; Creation Stories; Guru Nanak and the Sikh Gurus; Hindu Stories; The Life of the Buddha; The Life of Jesus; The Life of Mohammed; The Lives of the Saints* and *Old Testament Stories.* (S/T)

Religious Topics Series. London: Wayland Publishers Ltd., 1986.
There are eighteen books in this series, each covering key elements, customs and practices of the major religious traditions. Titles in this series are: *Birth Customs; Death Customs; Feasting and Fasting; Holy Books; Initiation Rites; Marriage Customs; Pilgrimage; Religious Buildings; Religious Dress; Religious Services; Teachers and Prophets; Family Life; Religious Art; Religious Beliefs; Religious Festivals; Religious Foods; Religious Symbols* and *The History of Religions.* (S/T)

Schuman, Jo Miles. *Art from Many Hands.* Boston: Davis Publications, 1984.
A valuable resource to help children discover the arts and crafts of many cultures. (T)

Teacher, they called me a _____. Prejudice and Discrimination in the Classroom. New York and Toronto: Anti-Defamation League of B'nai Brith, 1987.
An excellent resource, complete with activities, to help children learn about and combat prejudice and discrimination with regard to disabilities, race and ethnicity, appearance, religion, gender and life-style. (T)

Tharlet, Eve. *The Little Cooks.* Geneva: UNICEF.
An illustrated, step by step cookbook for children, featuring thirty-six international recipes, using everyday foods, along with hints for healthy eating and kitchen safety. (S/T)